APPALACHIAN ADVENTURE

APPALACHIAN ADVENTURE

FROM GEORGIA TO MAINE—
A Spectacular Journey on the Great American Trail

By the staffs of

The Atlanta Journal-Constitution

The News & Observer of Raleigh

The *Pittsburgh Post-Gazette*

The Hartford Courant

The *Maine Sunday Telegram*

LONGSTREET PRESS
Atlanta, Georgia

Published by
LONGSTREET PRESS, INC.
A subsidiary of Cox Newspapers,
A subsidiary of Cox Enterprises, Inc.
2140 Newmarket Parkway
Suite 118
Marietta, GA 30067

Printed in the United States of America

Electronic film prep and separations by Advertising Technologies, Inc., Atlanta, GA

1st printing, 1995

Library of Congress Catalog Card Number: 95-77253

ISBN: 1-56352-234-9

Jacket and book design by Jill Dible

Cover photo: *Mount Katahdin, the northern terminus of the Appalachian Trail, as seen from the West Branch of the Penobscot River in Maine.* Photo by John Patriquin, Maine Sunday Telegram

Back cover photo: *Hikers head down a trail in New Hampshire's White Mountains in late afternoon.* Photo by John Ewing, Maine Sunday Telegram

TABLE OF CONTENTS

This book could not have happened without the supreme efforts of a number of editors, graphic artists and other staff members working behind the scenes at each of the five newspapers participating in the project. Longstreet Press is indebted to the following people for their dedication and talents:

At *The Atlanta Journal-Constitution*: assistant features editor, Elizabeth Lee; assistant managing editor in features, Susan Soper; Sunday news editor, Phil Gast; and assistant systems editor, Frank Tedards.

At *The News & Observer* of Raleigh: state editor, Ben Estes; photo editor, Gene Furr; and section editor, Joe Miller.

At the *Pittsburgh Post-Gazette*: science editor, Byron Spice; and graphic artist, Stacy Innerst.

At *The Hartford Courant*: deputy metropolitan editor, Vic Kodis, who was instrumental in the creation of the newspaper series, An Appalachian Adventure; deputy managing editor, Pam Luecke; director of photography, Thom McGuire; and senior designer, Phil Lohman.

At the *Maine Sunday Telegram*: executive news editor, Curt Hazlett; graphics editor, Rick Wakely; and photographer, Jack Milton.

B Y   G A Y L O R D   N E L S O N

Shortly after my arrival in Washington as a freshman Senator in 1963, a gentleman named Dr. Cecil Cullander introduced himself to me at a reception. He said he understood that I had an interest in environmental issues and wondered if I could spare a few moments to talk about the future of the Appalachian Trail.

I could indeed. Though I had never hiked the trail itself, I had read enough about it over the years to know that the Appalachian Trail—like Yosemite National Park or Yellowstone National Park—was a rare gem, one of our environmental treasures. Now I learned from my new acquaintance that the great trail, stretching 2,158 miles from Maine to Georgia, was in desperate trouble. He pointed out that while much of the trail crossed public lands (most of them in national forests, though a significant stretch of the trail traversed Great Smoky Mountains National Park), many parts crossed private lands and existed there only at the sufferance of the landowners. Increasingly, as land ownership had changed hands over the years, many of the new owners had objected to the trail crossing their property and had closed off segments to the public. It was Dr. Cullander's conviction that at the current rate of trail closures, it would only be another 25 or 30 years before the Appalachian Trail virtually disappeared as an integrated unit. In his view, it would take an act of Congress to permanently establish and preserve the trail.

The next morning, I called in my legislative staff and directed them to begin drafting legislation that would preserve the trail. It was a formidable challenge. Among other things, legislation would involve the acquisition by the government of numerous parcels of private land scattered along the 2,000 miles of the trail as it wound its way through 14 states. Nevertheless, a bill was prepared, and in 1964 I introduced it as the Appalachian Trails Act.

In the meantime, sentiment for the establishment of other trails had been growing around the country. "We are spending billions for our new highways," a 1962 Outdoor Recreation Resources Review Commission had written, "but few of them being constructed or planned make any provision for safe walking and cycling. Europe, which has even greater population densities, has much to teach us about building recreation into the environment.... Car ownership is rising all over Europe, but in the planning of their roads and the posting of them, Europeans make a special effort to provide for those who walk or cycle. Why not here?"

A good question, and in 1965 we introduced a National Hiking Trails bill as a kind of answer. It was my strong feeling that we had a much better chance of passing the National Trails bill if it specifically included protection of the Appalachian Trail, which had strong support within the Congress. Consequently, in 1966 we folded our Appalachian Trails legislation into the larger bill. In the meantime, President Lyndon B. Johnson took a personal interest in the subject, instructing Secretary of the Interior Stewart Udall to develop recommendations for a national system of trails. In 1968, after two years of the sort of complex legislative maneuvering typical of public lands legislation, Congress passed the National Trails System Act "in order to provide for the ever increasing outdoor recreation needs of an expanding population and in order to promote public access to, travel within, and enjoyment and appreciation of the open-air, outdoor areas of the Nation." The act estab-

lished the Appalachian Trail and the Pacific Crest Trail as the first segments of the National Scenic Trails System, authorized the study of 14 additional trails and empowered the secretaries of the Interior and of Agriculture to establish shorter, urban-oriented recreation trails. President Johnson signed the act on October 2, 1968. At the same time he signed the National Wild and Scenic Rivers Act as well as legislation establishing Redwoods National Park and North Cascades National Park. It was a banner day for the environment.

Benton MacKaye (rhymes with "sky") no doubt was more pleased than even I was by the protection given the Appalachian Trail with passage of the National Trails System Act—as he should have been. The Appalachian Trail was his brainchild. A regional planner for both the Tennessee Valley Authority and the U.S. Forest Service during the course of his long life (he died in 1976 at the age of 96), MacKaye formally proposed the idea for the trail in the *Journal of the American Institute of Architects* in 1921, although he could never quite remember exactly when the idea had come to him. "It may have been in 1891," he once wrote, "while I was listening to bearded, one-armed Major John Wesley Powell recount to an enthralled audience in Washington City his historic trip through the Grand Canyon.... It may have been in 1897, in the White Mountains of New Hampshire, as Sturgis Pray and I struggled through a tangled blowdown.... Or it may have been in 1900 when I stood with another friend, Horace Hildreth, viewing the heights of the Green Mountains."

If he did not know exactly when he thought of the trail idea, he was never uncertain about why. The trail, he wrote, offered "a wilderness way through civilization, not a civilized way through the wilderness." It was a way to "absorb the landscape and its influence as revealed in the earth and primeval life," a place in which "to walk, to see, and to *see* what you see." Volunteers began cutting brush for the first segment of the "AT" (as the trail would become known) in 1923, and in 1925 a collection of hiking clubs and other trail-lovers established the Appalachian Trail Conference, a federation MacKaye put in context in his foreword to a National Geographic Society book, *The Appalachian Trail*, published in 1972:

> The creation of the Appalachian Trail Conference was one of the two pivotal events in the history of the trail; the other was the signing of the National Trails System Act in 1968. The first provided a parent organization for clubs whose members work at maintaining the trail; the second provided federal protection for it. Achieving this protected status is the result of the enthusiasm and concern of a host of hikers during half a century. Perhaps it is unrivaled by any other single feat in the development of American outdoor recreation.

It is entirely fitting that the collection of stories in *Appalachian Adventure* should appear in the 70th anniversary year of the creation of the Appalachian Trail Conference. I think that this book would have given Benton MacKaye special pleasure. For one thing, the idea behind it would have appealed to his sense of the unusual—indeed, the unique. I don't know of any gathering of stories and images quite like these in this book.

Moreover, I think MacKaye would be pleased that the stories capture in both text and photographs the same levels of enthusiasm that infected the AT's pioneer travelers and wonderfully evoke the varieties of experience that millions of hikers have found ever since. The Appalachian Trail remains one of the most popular outdoor recreation opportunities in the United States. Two-thirds of our population live within half-a-day's drive of one part or another of the AT. Yearly, three million people hike at least some part of the AT—and 2,000 people set out to hike *all* of it every year (though only about 170 make it all the way).

The AT is now almost complete—only about 38 miles of the trail remain unprotected—and for all the problems of continuing urban growth and its attendant pressures along much of its length, the trail stands as one of the great environmental success stories of the 20th century. Not as much can be said for the rest of the system authorized in 1968. While the 2,350-mile Pacific Crest Trail has now been completed, about 25,000 miles of designated scenic and historic trails have only been partially finished. That should be done, and I believe that individual states should expand and accelerate their own programs for trail development as well, for each new trail in an increasingly crowded world can show its own version of the "wilderness way through civilization" that Benton MacKaye envisioned for the AT. The Appalachian Trail still provides that singular gift. And, short of hiking off on your own, I can think of no better way to learn what the AT offers in the way of natural beauty, personal challenge and contact with the world beyond the concrete than to open this book and embrace what it gives you.

Gaylord Nelson
Counselor, The Wilderness Society

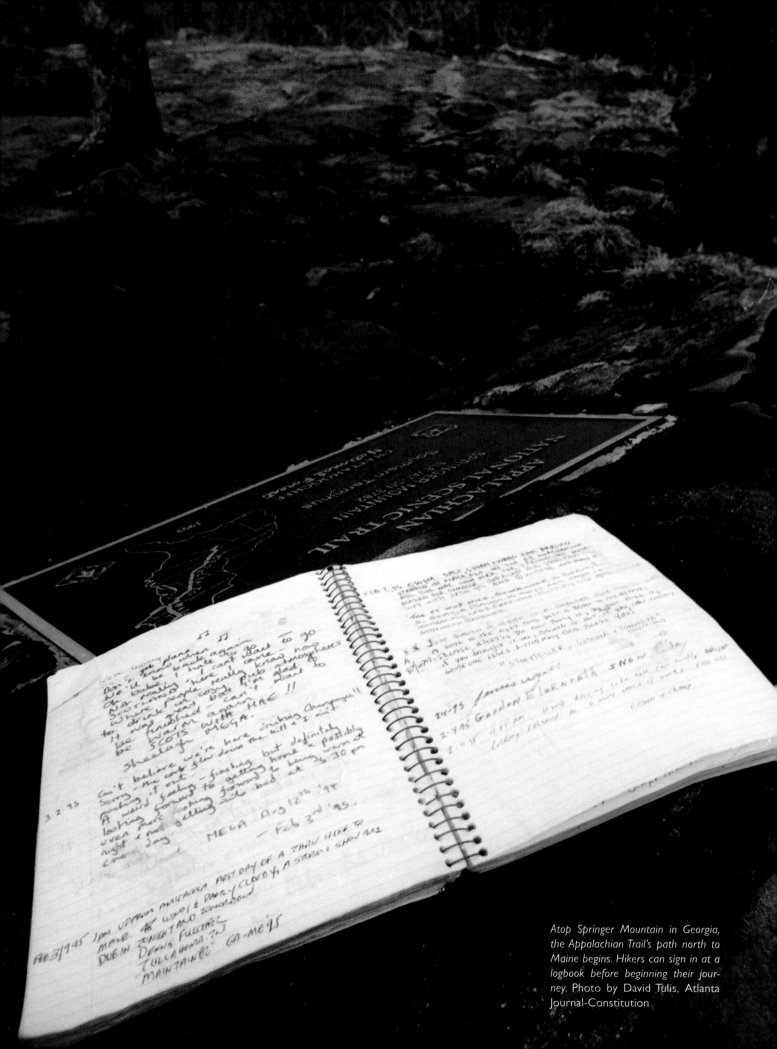

Atop Springer Mountain in Georgia, the Appalachian Trail's path north to Maine begins. Hikers can sign in at a logbook before beginning their journey. Photo by David Tulis, Atlanta Journal-Constitution

INTRODUCTION

BY ELIZABETH LEE

Journeys north on the Appalachian Trail begin atop Georgia's Springer Mountain, at a bronze plaque showing the silhouette of a man dressed in the hiking gear of 1934, a satchel slung purposefully over his right shoulder. "A footpath for those who seek fellowship with the wilderness," it reads.

Decades after the plaque was hammered into the rock of Springer Mountain, the Appalachian Trail continues to fulfill that pledge. Each year, up to four million people seek to get closer to nature on the world's longest marked footpath. Most are out just for the day; others, for a weekend camping trip or a week's journey. Far fewer are the through-hikers, who seek to traverse the trail's 2,158-mile-length in one season.

Joining these four million from March to October of 1995 were the members of An Appalachian Adventure team, a group of reporters, photographers and illustrators from five newspapers who walked the trail in relays. Their stories and images—-drawn from a series originally published in *The Atlanta Journal-Constitution*, *The News & Observer* of Raleigh, the *Pittsburgh Post-Gazette*, *The Hartford Courant* and the *Maine Sunday Telegram*—-appear on the following pages.

Like most of the 2,000 who set out to hike the entire trail in 1995, they began their journey on a rocky outcropping on Springer Mountain, where rural Appalachia has yet to succumb to the vacation-home-building boom sweeping the northeast Georgia mountains. Winter still clings to the southern Appalachians in early March, bringing the threat of snow and ice. The rigors of starting a 2,000-mile hike can be equally chilling: backpacks that weigh close to 50 pounds, muscle aches, isolation and the loss of creature comforts. Small wonder, then, that just 10 percent of those who intend to walk the length of the trail in one season actually do so.

The Appalachian Adventure team spent months readying themselves for the trail. On a practice hike, John Harmon surveys the mountains from Raven Rock Cliffs in North Carolina. Photo by David Tulis, Atlanta Journal-Constitution

The newspaper hike began with cheerful spirits and a camaraderie born of shared adventure and hardship. Soon after dawn on March 5, in a chilling 35° mist, the team signed the trail register and began a northbound journey that would take them through 14 states. On October 1, on a sunny Maine day when the thermometer reached an unseasonable 70°, the long trip ended atop Mount Katahdin with cognac toasts and a snack of Power Bars, energy food beloved by hikers.

▲

On their journey north, the group learned to do without familiar comforts and to battle anxieties. The hikers found solace in the silence of the woods and drew strength from spirit-lifting vistas atop rocky ridges.

It was this vision of spiritual renewal, along with a dash of utopianism, that spawned the creation of the Appalachian Trail. Forester and social reformer Benton MacKaye of Massachusetts, considered the father of the trail, envisioned it as a refuge for urbanites to refresh themselves in nature and as a footpath that would link a series of self-sufficient communities. He laid out his proposal in 1921, in the *Journal of the American Institute of Architects*. The communities never came to pass, but MacKaye's idea of a recreational retreat took hold, and in 1937, the final portion of the trail was completed on a Maine ridge. Volunteer hiking clubs, government agencies and workers in Depression-era programs such as the Civilian Conservation Corps built much of it; other sections were patched together from existing trails or placed along roads.

Other trailside communities have sprung up to replace the ones envisioned by MacKaye. Through-hikers form roving families and friendships that are nourished through messages in shelter registers and through their common goal. Many set out on the trail between life's passages—college graduates taking a break before settling down to a job, retirees fulfilling a life's dream, others seeking to escape the pain of a failed relationship or the death of a spouse. To mark their new identities, they take trail names such as Dances with Blisters and Mama Kazoo.

Some who live near the trail have formed communities tied into a backpacker's world, offering free lodging, cool drinks or a hot meal. Each spring, Tillie Wood of Roswell, Georgia, travels to central Virginia and opens a restored log building to hikers seeking a night's shelter. The Presbyterian Church of the Mountain in Delaware Water Gap, Pennsylvania, holds a weekly dinner for hikers and operates a basement hostel. Damascus, Virginia, known as the friendliest town on the trail, offers backpackers a hearty welcome and an annual festival, Trail Days, to coincide with the spring surge of northbound through-hikers. Harpers Ferry, West Virginia, is a touchstone, home to the Appalachian Trail Conference headquarters and the backpacking wisdom of "trail mother" Jean Cashin, who dispenses advice and deodorizing spray from her desk by the front door.

The Appalachian Trail Conference (ATC), formed in 1925, oversees the trail and the 32 clubs whose members maintain most of the footpath, in an unusual arrangement that gives responsibility for public land to a private organization. Club volunteers remove fallen trees, build new sections of trail, counter erosion and paint the 2-by-6-inch

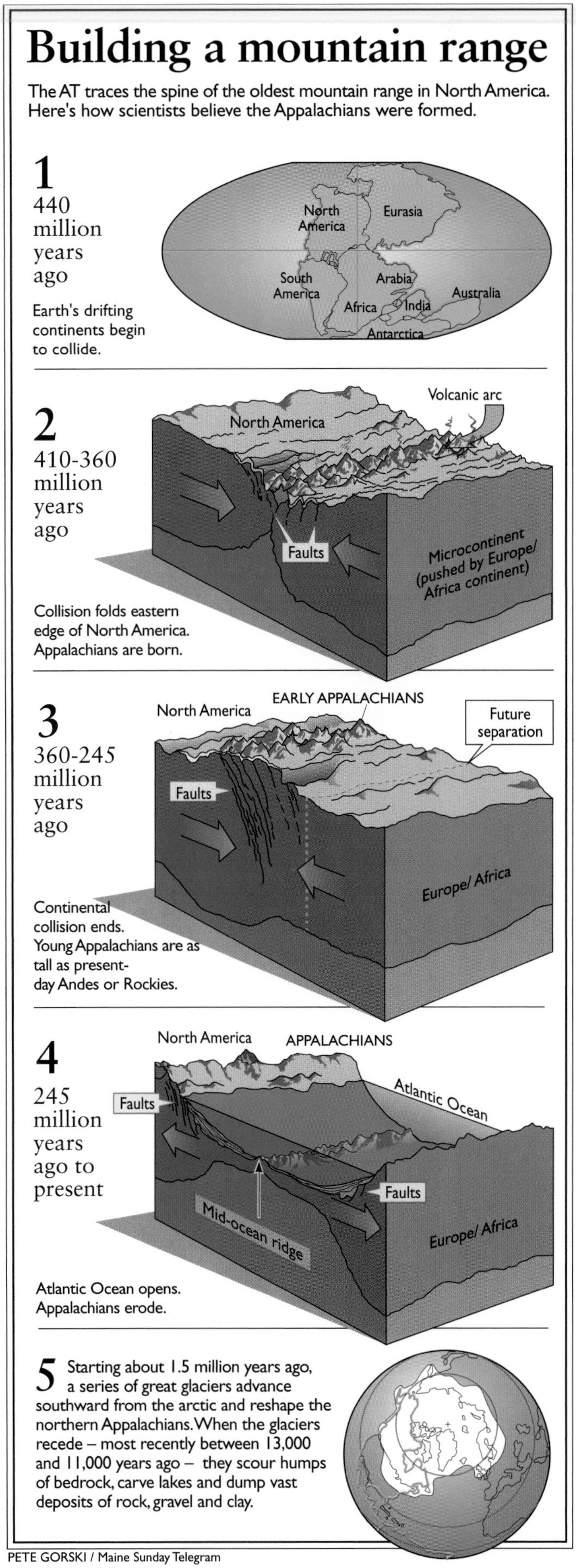

Building a mountain range

The AT traces the spine of the oldest mountain range in North America. Here's how scientists believe the Appalachians were formed.

1 440 million years ago

Earth's drifting continents begin to collide.

[diagram labeled: North America, Eurasia, South America, Arabia, Africa, India, Australia, Antarctica]

2 410-360 million years ago

Collision folds eastern edge of North America. Appalachians are born.

[diagram labeled: Volcanic arc, North America, Faults, Microcontinent (pushed by Europe/Africa continent)]

3 360-245 million years ago

Continental collision ends. Young Appalachians are as tall as present-day Andes or Rockies.

[diagram labeled: North America, EARLY APPALACHIANS, Future separation, Faults, Europe/Africa]

4 245 million years ago to present

Atlantic Ocean opens. Appalachians erode.

[diagram labeled: North America, APPALACHIANS, Atlantic Ocean, Faults, Mid-ocean ridge, Faults, Europe/Africa]

5 Starting about 1.5 million years ago, a series of great glaciers advance southward from the arctic and reshape the northern Appalachians. When the glaciers recede – most recently between 13,000 and 11,000 years ago – they scour humps of bedrock, carve lakes and dump vast deposits of rock, gravel and clay.

PETE GORSKI / Maine Sunday Telegram

Two father-and-son teams of backpackers head towards Hump Mountain (5,587 feet) out of Bradley Gap in Tennessee. Photo by Rob Cross, News & Observer

white blazes that keep hikers on the right track. The ATC also serves as a clearinghouse for information about the trail.

The footpath itself is constantly changing. In the past three decades, the trail has been partially rerouted as part of a government campaign to purchase a scenic corridor and protect it from development. Portions have been moved away from roads and in other cases relocated to more picturesque areas, away from factories and mountain vacation homes. By 1995, all but 43 miles of the trail were publicly owned. Meanwhile, other changes may lie ahead: One proposal calls for extending the trail into Canada, to Mount Jacques Cartier in Quebec, 420 miles from the trail's northern terminus on the top of Mount Katahdin.

As the trail's route has metamorphosed, so too has the way hikers approach it. As ever, day hikers drawn by easy access swell the ranks of visitors. But it's doubtful the footpath's creators envisioned the phenomenon of the through-hiker, which began when Pennsylvania author Earl Shaffer walked the length of the trail in 1948. Now, there are an estimated 200 through-hikers annually. Others tackle the trail in sections, devoting several days or weeks to notching new portions under their belts as they steadily amass the distance needed to join the ranks of 2,000-milers.

Wilderness along the trail can be illusory; in many areas outside national forests and

Cam-Ranh Chandler, 5, (bottom) tries to catch frogs in Finerty Pond in Massachusetts while her sisters, Viola, 6, (left) and Tiffany, 4, watch the action from a bog bridge over the pond. The three children were among the six children and teenagers in the Chandler family that were hiking with their mother for 100 miles, from Vermont to Connecticut. Photo by Michael Kodas, The Hartford Courant

The App

Harpers

Shenandoah
National Park

Damascus

Clingmans
Dome

WEST VIRGINIA

Springer Mountain

TENNESSEE

Knoxville Hot Springs

Fontana Villag

Pearisburg   Lynchburg

Richmond

VIRGINIA

Mt. Oglethorpe

Asheville

NORTH CAROLINA

Neels Gap

Great Smoky
Mountains
National Park

Charlotte   Raleigh

Atlanta

Columbia

GEORGIA

SOUTH CAROLINA

Sources: National Park Service/U.S. Dept. of the Interior

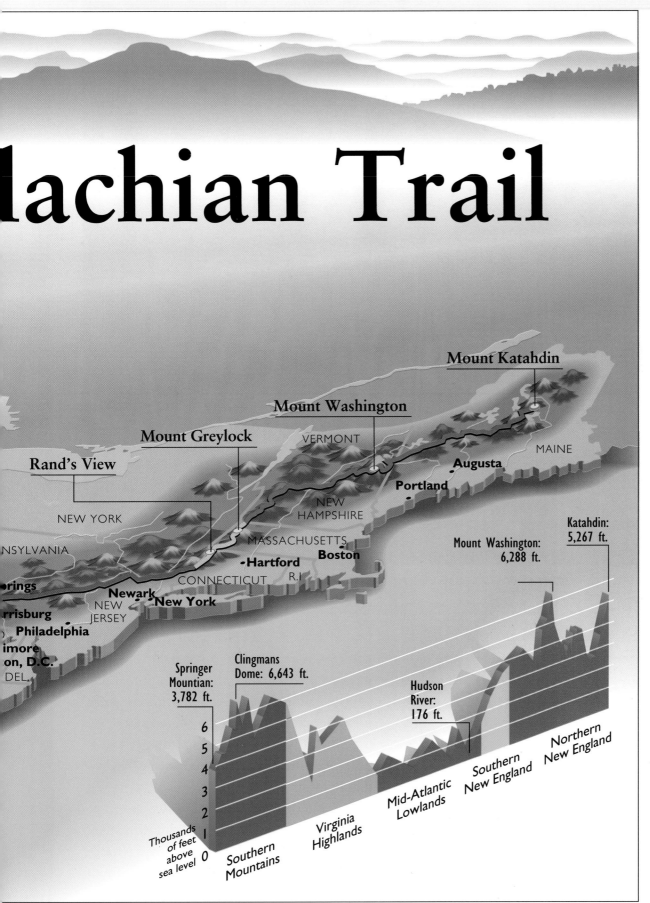

lachian Trail

Mount Katahdin

Mount Washington

Mount Greylock

VERMONT

MAINE

Rand's View

Augusta

Portland

NEW YORK

NEW
HAMPSHIRE

Katahdin:
5,267 ft.

NSYLVANIA

MASSACHUSETTS

Mount Washington:
6,288 ft.

Hartford

Boston

CONNECTICUT

R.I.

rings

Newark

New York

NEW
JERSEY

rrisburg

Philadelphia

imore

on, D.C.

DEL.

Springer
Mountian:
3,782 ft.

Clingmans
Dome: 6,643 ft.

Hudson
River:
176 ft.

6

5

4

3

2

Thousands
of feet
above
sea level

1

0

Southern
Mountains

Virginia
Highlands

Mid-Atlantic
Lowlands

Southern
New England

Northern
New England

KEN MOWRY and NAM NGUYEN / The News & Observer

A barred owl sits in a tree along the trail on Smarts Mountain in New Hampshire. Photo by Michael Kodas, The Hartford Courant

parks, only a 1,000-foot-wide swath serves as a scenic buffer. In other places, it's even narrower. Given that the Appalachian Trail lies within a day's drive of more than half the population of the United States, in an era when encountering wilderness means moving beyond the range of a cellular phone tower, it's surprising that the illusion endures. No matter that the occasional rumble of an interstate highway reaches hikers across the Valley of Virginia, or that ski resorts jostle with the trail in New England. For when tunnels of blooming rhododendrons funnel walkers through the southern Appalachians, or the

cry of a loon pierces a cool Maine night, nature reasserts itself as a constant.

The Appalachian Trail exerts a primal pull beyond the merely recreational. Many paths snake across portions of the United States, yet it is this ribbon traversing the country's eastern spine—-the first National Scenic Trail—- that holds an enduring fascination. Perhaps it beckons to the pioneer spirit buried in us, the desire to strike out for parts unknown, albeit with detailed guidebooks and way stations every few miles. Perhaps it's the lore of through-hikers such as Emma "Grandma" Gatewood, who, in her late 60s, walked the length of the trail in one season, then hiked it again, in the opposite direction, a couple of years later. Perhaps it's the romantic notion of discovering a bit of America by walking across the country and stumbling upon traces of early settlers—long-abandoned homesteads and overgrown orchards. Or maybe it's the sheer distance, scope and accessibility of the trail. Regardless, for many hikers, the storied Appalachian Trail promises adventure and the opportunity to experience a legend.

▲

"The Appalachian Trail. Those are magic words to anybody who has ever so much as spent a night sleeping in the woods," Paul Hemphill wrote in *Me and the Boy*, a 1986 account of hiking the trail with his 19-year-old son. "The 'AT' is Yankee Stadium and the Rose Bowl and the Kentucky Derby and the Grand Ole Opry...a test of strength and will and endurance that only 1,250 or so backpackers have conquered since both ends were connected in the mid-'30s."

For all of those reasons, and the desire to bring the story of the Appalachian Trail to their readers, five newspapers decided in 1994 to attempt a relay hike. After more than a year of planning and training, team members pulled on their boots, shouldered their packs and strode into the start of a great

Steve Grant takes a view from atop Cat Rock in southern New York near Greenwood Lake. The Appalachian Trail in New York traverses a series of "puddingstone" outcrops, which offer strenuous climbs and dramatic views. Photo by Michael Kodas, The Hartford Courant

Near the south fork of the Piney River, the trail snakes its way through a lushly carpeted forest floor. Photo by David Tulis, Atlanta Journal-Constitution

adventure. The journalists took sections of the trail, one team starting off as another finished its stint.

Bo Emerson, Dave Tulis, Walter Cumming and Chris Hunt of *The Atlanta Journal-Constitution* took the first leg through north Georgia and into the Great Smoky Mountains National Park, as the last vestiges of winter clung to the highlands. The wildflowers of spring—the Mayapple, trillium and columbine—burst into bloom as Scott Huler and Rob Cross of *The News & Observer* of

Raleigh walked across the balds of North Carolina and Tennessee and into southwestern Virginia. Pastoral landscapes and late spring flowers such as rhododendrons and lady's slippers greeted John Harmon, Paige Braddock, Dave Tulis and Martha Ezzard of *The Atlanta Journal-Constitution* as they hiked through central Virginia, where the trail wends its way through several small towns and skirts the Blue Ridge Parkway.

Summer had settled in by the time Don Hopey, Robin Rombach and Bill Wade of the

Secretary of the Interior Bruce Babbitt (right) takes a break to have a Klondike bar at the Loft Mountain Campstore with through-hiker David Heinstadt (Red Fox) of Baltimore, Maryland. Photo by Robin Rombach, Pittsburgh Post-Gazette

Pittsburgh Post-Gazette made their way from central Virginia to the Pennsylvania/New Jersey border, with Don battling a foot injury and rocky terrain but finding comfort in the warmth of residents and hiking friends he met along the way. As the relay hike moved into the crowded Northeast, Steve Grant, Mike Kodas and Susan Campbell of *The Hartford* *Courant* took over. A heat wave lingered as Steve and Mike walked through the valleys and oak-filled forests of New York and Connecticut and toward the birches and beeches of Vermont. Ski resorts still bustling in late summer greeted Susan as she picked up the trail and headed toward northern New Hampshire, the way growing steeper as she

The sun sets above a solitary tree on Big Bald in North Carolina. Photo by Rob Cross, News & Observer

Brilliant fall foliage blankets a hillside at Rainbow Ledges in the 100-mile wilderness. Photo by John Ewing, Maine Sunday Telegram

neared the White Mountains.

Lloyd Ferriss and John Ewing of the *Maine Sunday Telegram* toughed out a hike across some of the trail's most challenging territory, New Hampshire's Presidential Range, where the footpath goes above timberline, the winds are punishing and the climate harsh. Autumn was settling into the woods of central Maine when Edie Lau joined John to walk through the remote 100-mile wilderness, where northbound through-hikers get the first glimpse of their goal, Mount Katahdin. And at Baxter

A field of bluettes, one of the first spring flowers to bloom, grows along the trail. Photo by Rob Cross, News & Observer

State Park, most of the Appalachian Adventure team gathered once again, this time to walk the final miles and exult at the end of the trail on Katahdin's summit.

After the adventure ended, Don Hopey reflected on his experiences. "The culture I was exposed to, and that I became a part of after six weeks on the trail, was easily one of the best clubs that I've ever joined. It was really difficult to get back into the rhythm of civilization. It's a whole different rhythm out there on the trail."

Evening sun breaks through storm clouds to bathe Kinsman Mountain in New Hampshire while the rest of the White Mountains are covered with dark clouds. Photo by Michael Kodas, The Hartford Courant

Early morning light graces Mount Washington, viewed from along the trail in Pinkham Notch, New Hampshire. Photo by John Ewing, Maine Sunday Telegram

Many hikers advertise their past adventures with patches. This pack belongs to Susan Roquemore, who goes by the trail name of Dragon Lady. Photo by M. Chris Hunt, Atlanta Journal-Constitution

THE ADVENTURE BEGINS

M A R C H   5 - 2 5 ,   1 9 9 5

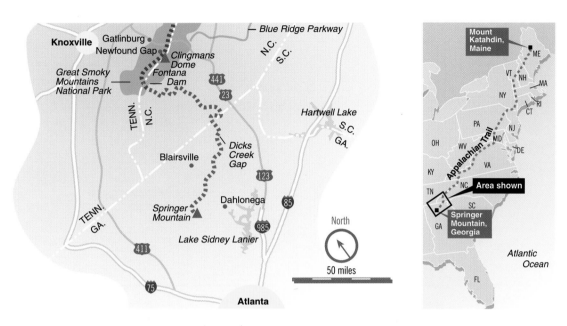

BLAIRSVILLE, GEORGIA

**Text by
Bo Emerson**

**Photography by
David Tulis**

Three days in, 31 miles down and 2,127 to go, I've taken my first big bite of this Appalachian Adventure, and I've discovered, as have many before me, that the Appalachians bite back.

It was 35° and misty as we began our hike atop Springer Mountain, the trail's southern terminus. Since then, we've had three days of rain, plentiful mud, steep trails, occasional frost, wet sleeping bags and soggy notebooks.

It's easy to see why only 10 percent of the 2,000 people who set out each spring to hike the Appalachian Trail from Georgia to Maine actually make it. Many quit in Georgia. Some give up during the 8-mile approach trail from Amicalola Falls, discarding their heavy cookware as they go.

"You could start an outfitter's store with

Bringing new meaning to the term "pack journalism," reporters and photographers from the five newspapers hiking the Appalachian Trail begin their 14-state odyssey atop Georgia's Springer Mountain, the trail's southern terminus. (From left, Scott Huler, Steve Grant, Don Hopey and Mike Kodas) **Photo by David Tulis, Atlanta Journal-Constitution**

The sound of Long Creek Falls beckons hikers down a short side trail. Photo by David Tulis, Atlanta Journal-Constitution

the gear people leave behind on the approach trail," Brian King, a spokesman for the Appalachian Trail Conference, told me before the hike began.

Though the terrain in Maine is steeper, the early spring weather in Georgia makes these miles the most forbidding for some hikers.

Being in these mountains, though, more than compensates for the inconvenience of being occasionally miserable. Despite the sloppy weather, certain moments were priceless. On the first day we strolled past Stover Creek and Long Creek Falls, where arching rhododendrons and ancient hemlocks transformed the soft pine-straw path into a glowing green tunnel. On the second night, photographer Dave Tulis and I stood on top of Big Cedar Mountain at sunset as the sky

cleared briefly and the peaks around Jacob's Knob rose from the surging clouds like black ships in a white sea.

As we set out on March 5 from Springer Mountain, journalists from all five newspapers involved in an Appalachian Adventure hiked together.

The defining moment came after we made a desperate camp on a muddy hillside that first night, with no drinkable water, a steady rain and not a dry pair of socks in the group.

Together we rigged a tarp, and Dave set a pot to catch runoff from the drooping edge. We boiled the last of our water for supper and, during a lull in the rain, yanked out our tents and inflated our sleeping pads. The rigors of 11.5 miles in the mud briefly forgotten, we savored after-supper coffee.

Debbielyn (Pearl Drops) Mills (center), her son James (Keebler) Milton, 12, (left) and Don Hopey take a break on Rich Mountain.
Photo by David Tulis, Atlanta Journal-Constitution

A fungus thrives on a downed tree limb near Stover Creek. Fallen trees occasionally block the trail, but they're soon cleared by volunteers who maintain the Appalachian Trail. Photo by David Tulis, Atlanta Journal-Constitution

Then photographer Mike Kodas produced a box of fudge from the nearby old mining town of Dahlonega. It might as well have been a box of Dahlonega gold.

Acknowledging the cheers, Kodas passed around the candy, saying, "You need things like this when it really sucks."

The beginning of our hike coincided with the season's first great wave of through-hikers bound for Maine, 14 states away. Many were in their 20s and 30s, taking time to realize a dream between graduation or jobs, but the lure of slipping out of civilization for a time appeals to even the youngest hikers. James Milton, 12, of Franklin County, Virginia, is playing hooky from the second half of seventh grade to hike the length of the trail with his mother, Debbielyn Mills, 36. His trail journal will become his English project for the year.

"It's been rough but good," said James (trail name: Keebler), hunkered in a sleeping bag at the Hawk's Mountain shelter, just 8 miles from Springer Mountain. His mother, who had picked up the trail name of Pearl Drops in honor of the six pearl studs in her left ear, was thankful that one son was still of an age to enjoy spending time with Mom. Her older son had opted to forgo the trip, staying home instead to get his driver's license.

Not everybody meets the challenge gracefully. Ben Carey, of Bethlehem, Connecticut, lamented that his hiking partner could only complain about the rain, the hills and the absence of that girlfriend back home. He worried that he'd be hiking alone before too much longer.

It's easy to understand why people quit. What's harder to understand is how they persevere.

The steep climb up Preacher's Rock on Big Cedar Mountain rewards hikers with a view of Jacob's Knob and clouds settling in for the evening. Photo by David Tulis, Atlanta Journal-Constitution

The trail runs right through the Walasi-Yi Center at Neels Gap, Georgia, a New Deal-era stone building now home to a backpacking store and hiker hostel owned by Jeff (pictured) and Dorothy Hansen. After writer Bo Emerson's boots came apart during his first three days on the trail, he stopped at Walasi-Yi for a replacement pair. Photo by David Tulis, Atlanta Journal-Constitution

Paul Coryea (Lucky Pierre), a retired engineer from Rome, Georgia, went the distance in 1992, despite an ankle injury sustained early on the trail, at Bly Gap, North Carolina.

As the press gang set out from Springer, Coryea, 61, walked along for a mile or so, moving briskly with the aid of two ski poles. He seemed to enjoy the freezing precipitation.

His advice was simple. "Be careful going down the hills," he said, "and when the going gets rough, remember, that will pass. You'll get a sunny day."

For the next 164 miles, I pray he's right.

Words of encouragement from Paul Coryea (Lucky Pierre), who through-hiked the trail in 1992, bolster the team's spirits as the journey north begins. Photo by David Tulis, Atlanta Journal-Constitution

RAINBOW SPRINGS, NORTH CAROLINA

Illustrations by Walter Cumming

The rain is gone, the skies are clear and my ears are getting sunburned. When it got clear, though, it also got cold. The temperature plunged to 15°, with a below-zero wind-chill. My water bottle froze. It snowed inside the tent from our condensed exhalations. My toothpaste, viscous as window putty, wouldn't squeeze out of the tube. But in my space-age polyester fleece jacket and my polypropylene long underwear, I stayed toasty warm. I'll never make fun of polyester again.

By noon the next day I was hiking in shorts and a T-shirt.

From Neels Gap, the Appalachian Trail meanders northeasterly, keeping to the ridge line of the Blue Ridge. From our campsite on

Near Georgia's Poplar Stamp Gap, early morning sunlight warms a wintry scene. Photo by David Tulis, Atlanta Journal-Constitution

the shoulder of Tray Mountain we saw the lights of Helen, a mock Bavarian village that's a magnet for North Georgia tourists, in the valley. That day, Dave left the trail and I was joined by illustrator Walter Cumming.

The next day, Walter and I turned toward the north and crossed above Lake Burton. We cooked black beans with garlic and onions on a bluff near Dicks Creek while listening to a barred owl question our campfire.

As we passed into North Carolina, the mountains got bigger. In Georgia, the trail rises above 4,000 feet only a few times, topping Blood, Tray and Rocky mountains, among others. But in North Carolina, 4,000 feet is the ground floor.

In the mountains, spring is still a rumor that the songbirds trade. I hear the Bradford pears are blooming in Atlanta, but here the landscape remains gray and brown, punctuated by the silver of birch and beech and the ever-present blue-green rhododendron.

The liveliest vegetation appeared between the breathtaking climbs up Standing Indian (5,498 feet) and Albert Mountain (5,250), where shiny-leafed galax plants thickly bordered the path for almost a quarter-mile.

Those climbs were a good deal easier, thanks to a 100-pound malamute named Chinook.

What a difference a dog makes.

Chinook belongs to Walter, whom the through-hikers call the Frenchman. (He's practicing the language for a trip to Quebec.) To my

It's 15° on this March morning—all the more reason to work up a sweat with a brisk uphill walk. David Heinstadt (from left), Ann Harris, Nan Sutton and Jason Sain are heading to Levelland Mountain, Georgia. Photo by David Tulis, Atlanta Journal-Constitution

discomfiture, I've been dubbed Young John Denver.

Walter, a friend since childhood, and Chinook are accompanying me as far as Wesser, North Carolina, another 30 miles up the trail. Chinook keeps camp-prowling varmints at bay, eats our dinner scraps (a

Silver Birch on Betty Creek

By Walter Cumming, Atlanta Journal-Constitution

big concern when you have to bury, burn or pack out any leftovers) and, most important, carries her own backpack, with about 10 pounds of gear, including our stove, fuel and extra clothes.

This makes my pack and my heart lighter, but also allows the

From Wolf Laurel Top, hikers get a glimpse of the Tennessee Valley Divide. Photo by David Tulis, Atlanta Journal-Constitution

Chinook, the hiking malamute, trained for six months before hitting the trail. When the going got rough, her owner, Walter Cumming, shouldered her pack. Dogs can accompany hikers almost everywhere on the Appalachian Trail, although they are forbidden in Great Smoky Mountains National Park. Photo by Walter Cumming, Atlanta Journal-Constitution

Frenchman to bring along fancy cookware, which he uses to produce mind-blowing, 5,000-calorie meals. On the day we met at Tray Gap, I was drained. My feet were size 9 chunks of pain. I was starving. Walter was sautéing vegetables for a tomato sauce. His first words were, "Can you eat a half pound of pasta? Do you like fresh bell peppers? Would you like some cabernet sauvignon with that?"

Yes.

Many hikers rely on freeze-dried or dehydrated food, such as soup, pasta and oatmeal, as staples of their diet because they are light, don't take up much room in a pack and are a ready source of carbohydrates. Canned tuna, peanut butter and trail mix (granola, raisins, nuts, M&Ms and other ingredients) add variety. Through-hikers typically restock weekly, buying perishables to eat on their first day back on the trail. Here, Walter Cumming sautés bell peppers and onions for a spaghetti dinner. Photo by David Tulis, Atlanta Journal-Constitution

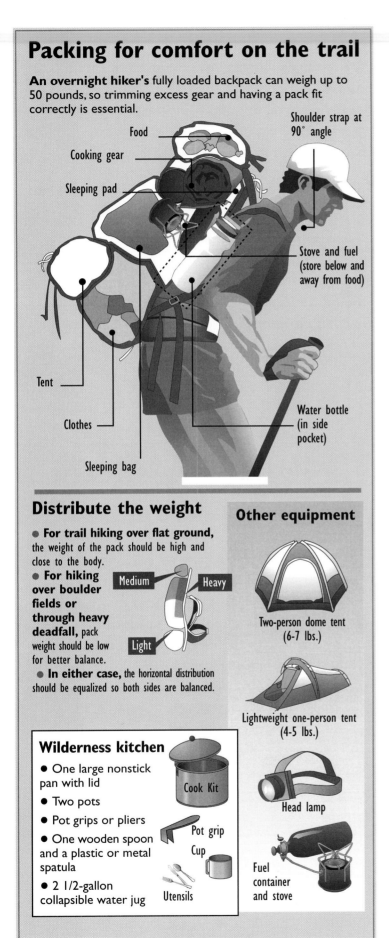

Packing for comfort on the trail

An overnight hiker's fully loaded backpack can weigh up to 50 pounds, so trimming excess gear and having a pack fit correctly is essential.

- Food
- Cooking gear
- Sleeping pad
- Shoulder strap at 90° angle
- Stove and fuel (store below and away from food)
- Tent
- Clothes
- Water bottle (in side pocket)
- Sleeping bag

Distribute the weight

- **For trail hiking over flat ground,** the weight of the pack should be high and close to the body.
- **For hiking over boulder fields or through heavy deadfall,** pack weight should be low for better balance.
- **In either case,** the horizontal distribution should be equalized so both sides are balanced.

Medium / Heavy / Light

Other equipment

Two-person dome tent (6-7 lbs.)

Lightweight one-person tent (4-5 lbs.)

Head lamp

Fuel container and stove

Wilderness kitchen

- One large nonstick pan with lid
- Two pots
- Pot grips or pliers
- One wooden spoon and a plastic or metal spatula
- 2 1/2-gallon collapsible water jug

Cook Kit

Pot grip

Cup

Utensils

STEPHEN CAMPER/ Atlanta Journal-Constitution

Walter believes that good food makes the difference between average hiking and great hiking. While the quality of the Frenchman's cooking is probably unequaled among the through-hikers we've met, these hikers have all matched us in volume eaten.

Hikers eat an ungodly amount of food, and yet they still burn more calories (426 an hour) than they can consume. Hauling weight up and down hills kicks the metabolism into overdrive and turns hikers into human Hoovers.

Walter, a marathon runner and a graduate of Wyoming's rigorous National Outdoor Leadership School, understands mountains. In fact, he says the best way to get in shape

Old-growth trees are rare in the Appalachians, which were farmed and heavily logged once. Hikers such as Ann Harris (pictured) are more likely to walk through second- and third-growth forests, such as these found at Georgia's Low Gap. In north Georgia and North Carolina, where much of the trail runs through national forests, logging continues in some areas. Photo by David Tulis, Atlanta Journal-Constitution

By Walter Cumming, Atlanta Journal-Constitution

for hiking isn't by doing wind sprints or push-ups. To get in shape, says Walter, get fat.

Even so, few hikers allow themselves the luxury of that extra frying pan. Backpackers are like foot-powered space capsules, carrying the essentials to support life and little

more. I've heard of a through-hiker who sawed the handle off his toothbrush to save weight.

Yet most hikers take something extra, a nonessential item for pleasure or comfort. I have a polished purple stone that my seven-year-old daughter Molly gave me. "I stored up hope in it," she said.

North Carolinian Jason Sain (Yak), 23, eating a summer sausage lunch at Tesnatee Gap, Georgia, held up his luxury item, a non-descript pebble taken from the trail's end at Mount Katahdin, Maine.

A friend gave it to him, saying, "When you're feeling depressed, and you want to quit, take it out, and say to yourself, 'I've got to take it home.'"

Photography by
M. Chris Hunt

FONTANA DAM, NORTH CAROLINA

It has been a mind-boggling experience to climb through these mountains, to live in wildness within sight of city lights and to realize that one can, with a little determination, walk 160 miles. But the biggest surprise has been the discovery of the Appalachian Trail's traveling society, a culture of modern-day hoboes who have their own language, clothing, rituals and diet. They hike not just for "fellowship with the wilderness," as the plaque on Springer Mountain claims, but to reaffirm their connection with each other.

In other words, the Appalachian Trail is not just a solitary deep-woods experience, said Bob Gallimore (Duct Tape), of Salinas, California. "It's a superhighway," he said, "but a nice superhighway."

Keebler studied with tutors at night to make up for missing school while hiking the trail. He's keeping a journal for a school project. Photo by David Tulis, Atlanta Journal-Constitution

Hikers share food, money and even muscle, occasionally hefting a pack for a tired or injured friend. Groups coalesce at night around the fire rings, where members exchange stories and songs, and log entries in the shelter registers.

"It's like a party that moves up the Appalachians," said Lance Holland, special projects manager at the Fontana Village Resort, a one-time home to World War II-era workers on North Carolina's Fontana Dam.

The resort has become a regular stopping place for hikers preparing for the 70-mile trip through the Great Smoky Mountains. They catch a shower, perhaps a room, and pick up parcels at the post office. From here, photographer Chris Hunt and I are tying on our boots for the last leg of our section of the trip. The rustic resort's better-groomed customers and the scruffy through-hikers who congregate here seem to coexist happily.

Like the Nantahala Outdoor Center, where Walter, Chinook and I parted company several days ago, Fontana Village is one of many off-trail elements of the hiker's extended world.

Within this world hikers come together in ad hoc units that withstand long miles and hard stress. "We were sitting around having dinner and I thought to myself, I can't believe I've only known these people two weeks," said Pearl Drops.

"I think of Debbie and Jamie and Kathi as my family," said Ben Carey (Sparrow Hawk), 20.

Jason Sain checks out "Doonesbury" after receiving the comics in a care package in Fontana Village, North Carolina. Photo by M. Chris Hunt, Atlanta Journal-Constitution

A case in point: Ben retraced his steps over Courthouse Bald to carry Kathi Georgitis' pack when she was discouraged by blisters and her hiking partner's decision to drop out.

By Walter Cumming, Atlanta Journal-Constitution

By Walter Cumming, Atlanta Journal-Constitution

Bo filing story 6:30 a.m. at Rainbow Springs cabin

NEWFOUND GAP, TENNESSEE

The Smoky Mountains: the crown of the Appalachian Trail, where the immense and ancient slopes of the second-highest mountains in the East are topped with grassy Alpine fields speckled with purple spring beauties; a wilderness with more species of trees than the continent of Europe; a paradise where I stop to fill my water bottle and share the spring with bold deer and timid copperheads.

The Smoky Mountains: where 8.6 million visitors pumped their auto exhaust into the air last year; where my 12-person shelter is jammed with 20 snoring campers; where I see a hiker wash his hair and dishes in the spring where I've drawn my drinking water.

Here the good and bad of the Appalachian Trail come together. Despite the traffic, the Great Smoky Mountains National Park remains largely unscarred, through strict controls and wise stewardship of back-country sites.

This is indeed an inaccessible stretch of the Appalachian Trail. As it traverses the 71-mile

Later, Kathi, dubbed "Swiss Miss" for her blond braids, carried Chris Gallagher's (Gingerbread Man's) pack when he tore a back muscle.

I have been helped many times by "trail angels"—those who live near the trail or visit often to help hikers—who bring beer, food, Power Bars, encouragement and good cheer. I met Jim and Betty Weiland just after they'd taken a through-hiker nicknamed White Root to an orthopedist to check out his bad knee. Retired to Franklin, North Carolina, from Atlanta, the couple didn't know the young man but had learned of his plight through the grapevine.

"We like hikers," said Betty, who stopped by Rainbow Springs Campground, another off-trail fixture near Franklin, to find me.

It's experiences like this, said Gallimore, puffing on a cigarette at the Carter Gap, North Carolina, shelter, that make the trail hard to forget.

"Once you hike a long way on this trail," he said, "you dig a groove in your memory that you trip over every day."

A spring beauty heralds the arrival of a new season. Photo by M. Chris Hunt, Atlanta Journal-Constitution

Looking north at Thunderhead Mountain from Spence Field, Bo Emerson scans the route he will take along the spine of the Great Smoky Mountains. Photo by M. Chris Hunt, Atlanta Journal-Constitution

spine of the park, following the Tennessee-North Carolina state line southwest to northeast, the trail crosses a road only once. Volunteers must hike a full day to clear downed trees in certain sections.

But I didn't mind doing the limbo under those deadfalls. Because when the day-hikers departed and I was alone with the resinous, fragrant evergreens, I felt as remote from the 20th century as Eden is from Atlanta. There were moments in the windless sunshine above Double Spring Gap so preternaturally quiet I could hear the pause before the great vernal overture, the world at attention, awaiting

God's downbeat. To move my feet was a rudeness. I stood still.

The Smoky Mountains are the most successful of national parks, as the Appalachian Trail is the most successful of national trails, and success can cause problems: erosion, trash, air pollution, overcrowding.

The Smokies are safe from at least one threat: clear-cuts. While national forests further south on the trail are open to commercial logging, it's not permitted in national parks. From the grass-topped mountains 40 miles south of Fontana Dam, I saw acres of those bare patches that call to mind the scalped

Sid Duncan (Dances with Blisters), makes it to the top of Rockytop Mountain in the Great Smoky Mountains. Photo by M. Chris Hunt, Atlanta Journal-Constitution

flanks of a dog ready for surgery.

Most of the hikers I met regard clear-cuts as an abomination. One, who goes by the trail name of Big Al, decided to stage a rebellion. He earned the name by vowing to destroy a Forest Service sign describing the benefits of clear-cuts that once stood on the summit of Albert Mountain, North Carolina. Hours before I topped Albert's rocky slopes, Big Al sawed through the sign's wooden posts and dropped it off the precipice.

Within a day Big Al became a trail legend, but he met with swift justice. He was turned in by another hiker and buttonholed by U.S. Forest Service officials when he reached the Nantahala River. (He returned on April 12 to Bryson City, North Carolina, where he received a suspended six-month prison sentence, was fined $250 and ordered to pay $750 in restitution to the National Forest Service. In addition, he was placed under a year's probation, during which time he is barred from the National Parks and National Forests of western North Carolina without the approval of his probation officer.)

Big Al is actually mild-mannered 21-year-old Graham Balch from Sandy Springs, Georgia, a college student of average height and serious intent. "They threatened me with not being able to go on any Forest Service land for a long time," said the young man when I caught up with him on Cheoah Bald in late March. "That would kill me right there."

Graham sighed. "I guess that's the end of my monkey-wrenching."

I felt a twinge of sympathy. But the

A new awareness:
Low-impact camping

Care of a wilderness environment is not a new concept. It is as old as Henry David Thoreau and St. Francis. However …

What is new is the annual invasion of an estimated 4 million pairs of lug-soled boots and the impact of the outdoor recreation boom on the Appalachian Trail. Responsible hikers pride themselves on minimizing the ongoing damage caused by 60 years of hiking. For more information on low impact camping, read *Soft Paths* by Bruce Hampton and David Cole (Stackpole, $10.95), or call the National Outdoor Leadership School in Lander, Wyoming, at (800) 332-4100. Here are tips from the National Outdoor Leadership School:

DO	WHY
▶ Select a campsite away from hiking trail or game trails, 100 feet from water sources and preferably in a timbered area away from meadows. Don't move rocks or logs or dig trenches.	▶ Big game are dangerous when startled. Wind can fell a dead tree. Meadows are fragile ecosystems. It can take hundreds of years for a landscape altered by man to return to its natural state.
▶ Use a stove for cooking. Use existing fire rings only. Avoid overused campsites where wood is already scarce. Don't break branches from logs or trees. Burn all food scraps or pack them out.	▶ Campfires permanently scar a wilderness unless great care is taken. Charcoal lasts thousands of years. Broken branches scar the beauty of a campsite. Buried or unburned food will attract insects, rodents and snakes.
▶ Dig a small latrine about 6 inches deep (at least 100 feet from water source, trail or camp) for human waste. Try to save a sod block or carefully moved log or rock to return to that spot. Burn used toilet paper.	▶ Any variance from this technique is a severe insult to a wilderness, aesthetically and biologically. Animals will dig up buried toilet paper.

In the first light of day, a deer rests in the forest near Spence Field Shelter. Photo by M. Chris Hunt, Atlanta Journal-Constitution

clear-cuts that mutilated the view from Wayah Bald, North Carolina, didn't make me as angry as the used toilet paper and feces I found above ground at a campsite near the summit. The trail is littered with such ugliness, a sign of thoughtless hikers who care little for those who follow in their footsteps.

There was other ugliness on the trail. Atop Clingmans Dome, the trail's highest point at 6,643 feet, Fraser firs weakened by acid rain have been stripped to the bones by a European aphid. Walking to the top of the observation tower, I was suspended in an eerie forest of bone-white tree skeletons.

The forest looks fragile here. But before I could ask whether the woods would survive, my own well-being came into question.

At the end of my second-to-last day in the park, I ran off the trail. I knew I'd gone wrong and made a foolish bid to bushwhack to the next white blaze that would mark the trail. I found myself a quarter-mile down a muddy vertical stream bed in the near-dark, and discouraged. Equal parts fear and embarrassment whipped me back up the hill. How easy to get eaten by the woods, I thought. I celebrated my escape that night with wild onions in my rice. I was reassured, reminded that in contests between humans and mountains, the mountains win.

RIGHT: *The trail through Spence Field in Great Smoky Mountains National Park shows signs of overuse. As hikers wear down a path, water runoff and erosion exacerbate the problem.* Photo by M. Chris Hunt, Atlanta Journal-Constitution

BELOW: *The skeletons of giant firs make the view from Clingmans Dome as ghastly as it is breathtaking. The balsam woolly adelgid, a European insect, caused the damage.* Photo by M. Chris Hunt, Atlanta Journal-Constitution

A curious whitetail deer takes a break from feeding just below the summit of Clingmans Dome in Great Smoky Mountains National Park. Photo by Rob Cross, News & Observer

CHASING SPRING

M A R C H   2 4 - M A Y   9 ,   1 9 9 5

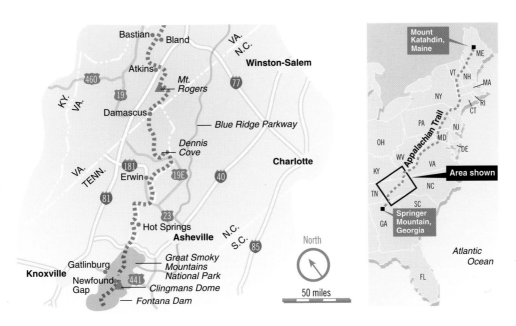

NEWFOUND GAP
TENNESSEE

**Text by
Scott Huler**

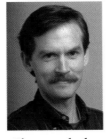

**Photography by
Rob Cross**

The spiral-bound trail register at the Fontana Dam shelter contained a message, left on March 18, from "Sleeper."

"Don't give up," Sleeper wrote. "Slow down a little now... Believe me, the adventure is worth the adversity!"

Heading north from Fontana, AT hikers find plenty of adversity as they enter the Great Smoky Mountains National Park. For the first three hours, the trail climbs 2,000 feet to the top of Shuckstack (4,020 feet), where a fire tower affords a spectacular view for the price of another few dozen footsteps.

Two days later, hikers reach Clingmans Dome, at 6,643 feet the highest point on the trail. The drop to Newfound Gap (5,045 feet) offers little relief for hikers who have climbed, when each peak and gap is totaled, some 9,000 feet in four days.

So as we started walking, Sleeper's advice was very much on our minds. Less than 200 miles into the 2,158-mile Appalachian Trail, at least 15 percent of hopeful through-hikers have called it quits.

For photographer Rob Cross and me, even during those arduous climbs, delight and surprise banished thoughts of quitting.

At the Russell Field shelter, for example, we found Mike Toomey, a Knoxville, Tennessee, teacher of Appalachian history, who told us to look out for Hop's Rock, a boulder just past the bald at Rockytop (5,441 feet).

The Smokies, which became a national park in 1934, have seen their share of cattle

Dropping off: Why hikers quit the trail

In its 58-year history only about 3,000 have hiked the entire Appalachian Trail—about 10 percent of those who started out. The four main reasons for quitting:

60%—Run out of will; find hiking day after day is not what they thought it would be or they don't have sufficient stamina.

25%—Run out of money.

10%—Run out of time; other commitments arise or their pace is slower than they expected.

5%—Become injured or get sick.

Taking its toll: How far do they get?

Percent remaining at various points on the trail

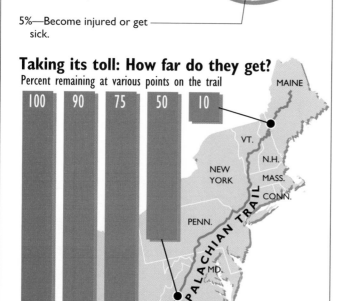

100 90 75 50 10

MAINE
VT.
N.H.
NEW YORK
MASS.
CONN.
PENN.
APPALACHIAN TRAIL
MD.
VA.
NORTH CAROLINA
SOUTH CAROLINA
GEORGIA

Information provided by Dan Bruce (Wingfoot), founder of the Center for Appalachian Trail Studies and author of The Thru-Hiker's Handbook.

TOM MOSIER / The News & Observer

Looking off towards Mount Mitchell, North Carolina, the highest point on the eastern seaboard, from the observation deck atop Clingmans Dome (6,643 feet), the highest point on the Trail. The dead trees below are Fraser firs, killed by a combination of pollution and the balsam woolly aphid. **Photo by Rob Cross, News & Observer**

breathtaking. Tiny, pale-blue bluets and white-and-crimson spring beauties carpeted the woods, and what the birds lacked in volume they made up for in variety: Rob's keen eyes picked out a pileated woodpecker and a golden-crowned kinglet. And when we connected a short, clear song we had been hearing for days with a solitary vireo—one of the first spring birds of the Appalachians—it lifted our spirits for hours. We were both also relieved to be able to identify a strange thrumming noise we'd heard as the call of a ruffed grouse, not the thumping of our hearts.

In Gatlinburg, Tennessee, to resupply, we stopped at the Happy Hiker outfitter, where our Polaroids were added to the 23 already tacked to the wall. The Appalachian Trail class of 1995 already far outstrips the classes of 1994 and 1993, which had only 16 at this point.

Lee Lewis, the store's manager, has seen a lot of hikers succeed and fail. It's a matter of attitude, he said. Out on the trail, "there's

grazing. Hop Harris was probably a herder during the late 1800s and early 1900s, Toomey said, who carved his name and initials in the boulder each year he made the trek. Rob and I had a sunny lunch on the rock, eating in silence as we looked out over ridge upon ridge of mountains disappearing into the Smokies' characteristic blue haze.

Even in a dry March, the Appalachian Trail in the Smokies is almost never short of

A Boy Scout troop from Birmingham, Alabama, out on spring break heads south from Clingmans Dome. Photo by Rob Cross, News & Observer

The most common early spring flower along the ridge crest of the Smokies is the spring beauty, which sometimes blankets the grasses near the trail like late snow. Photo by Rob Cross, News & Observer

nothing except trees to gripe to, and rocks to kick." The hikers are out there on their own. Not all of them like it.

The ones who succeed, he said, "have the vision of making it. They can see themselves there."

As for us, we're listening to Sleeper. And we're trying to keep the vision.

▲ **TRAIL MIX—**
Most through-hikers are three weeks into the trail now, and trail names have completely supplanted previous identities. I was named Curly by our old pal Keebler, the 12-year-old who's hiking the trail with his mom, Pearl Drops; Rob has adopted "Strider," though he doubts that he's the first Strider on the trail. An Appalachian Adventure as a whole is being called "the Geraldo Group" by through-hikers. We would never suggest that our

Atlanta colleagues, who logged the first stretch of trail, did anything to earn this sobriquet. ▲

HOT SPRINGS, NORTH CAROLINA

Atop the wooden sign marking where the Appalachian Trail leaves Great Smoky Mountains National Park sat a rock. Beneath the rock, folded several times, was a green piece of paper torn from a stenographer's notebook. As I lifted the rock I saw that the paper bore my trail name: Curly.

It was from Keebler.

Rob and I hadn't seen Keebler—or Pearl Drops—since we rejoined the trail for our portion of An Appalachian Adventure at Fontana Dam nearly two weeks earlier, though we had been reading the notes they left in shelter registers a day or so ahead of us. We sent greetings forward with faster hikers, but this was the first time we had gotten a response.

A red squirrel on patrol during the dinner hour at the Pecks Corner shelter in Great Smoky Mountains National Park. These squirrels are found in higher elevations in the Appalachians. Photo by Rob Cross, News & Observer

A deadfall in the Smokies gives one trail maintainer a chance to display a little chainsaw wizardry. Photo by Rob Cross, News & Observer

"Dear Curly, I got your message...I'm looking forward to seeing you. Smokies were hard but I made it and I'm not going to stop. Keebler."

Keebler's note was the high point of our week, not that it required extra high points. Starting from Newfound Gap, which straddles the North Carolina–Tennessee border, we hiked through beautiful weather in wild terrain. Whereas the eastern portion of the Smokies was majestic, filled with long views and parades of stately ridges, the western half of the park was spectacular. The first day north from Newfound Gap brought us to Charlies Bunion (5,375 feet), an iron-stained

LEFT: *Spring hikers climb Charlies Bunion, a rock outcropping north of Newfound Gap in the Smokies.* Photo by Rob Cross, News & Observer

BELOW: *From Newfound Gap north and east to Davenport Gap, the trail through Great Smoky Mountains National Park is graded, courtesy of the 1930s Civilian Conservation Corps.* Photo by Rob Cross, News & Observer

outcropping of the Smokies' characteristic slate, from which the Tennessee Mountains stretched so far beneath an azure sky that we could see the Cumberland Plateau beyond.

The trail in the Smokies never dipped much below that scenic level. Often, it traversed 5,000-foot-high ridges only a few feet wide—where a rock dropped on either side would tumble hundreds of feet—and the mountains seemed to jockey for our attention, offering the rushy green of heath balds, meadows, strips of verdant pine

After a night of freezing temperatures, the warmth of the morning sun just north of the Pecks Corner shelter starts the daily thaw of icicles at a hillside spring. Photo by Rob Cross, News & Observer

on dry slopes, and the sudden appearance of blooming redbuds and the white puffs of serviceberry trees. The trail along the State Line Branch, just north of the Smokies, was almost impossibly beautiful. Water cascaded over huge moss-backed boulders; hemlocks and rhododendrons leaned over chilly pools where long-legged water striders skated.

Amazingly, our meetings were few—just day hikers or college students on spring break. We seemed to have hit a seam in through-hiker traffic.

George Ziegenfuss (Ziggy) of western Virginia leaves the Roaring Fork shelter with a full pack early in the morning. Photo by Rob Cross, News & Observer

An old-style trail marker still hangs on a sign near the Roan High Knob shelter, elevation 6,000 feet. Photo by Rob Cross, News & Observer

Of the through-hikers we did meet, one thing was no longer on their minds: equipment. Initially, hikers endlessly compared packs—internal versus external frame—stoves, sleeping bags and boots as though certain that their gear held the key to outdoor success. By now, nearly 300 miles into their hikes, they realized that people had been surviving outdoors since long before there were doors to be out of. Earl Shaffer, who completed the first solo through-hike in 1948, carried not much more than a poncho, food, clothes and cooking gear. He didn't even keep a tent.

Rob and I shared a shelter one night with Daniel Harris and Chris Rivard, two University of Georgia students. They relaxed in camp chairs and, like most hikers, wore polar fleece made from recycled soda bottles and sported backpacks that cost several hundred dollars and held nearly 60 pounds of gear.

Harris, thinking about his stuff, smiled wryly when he was asked about campers who believe that without Gore-Tex they'd die before lunch. "I don't think you even need one of these packs," he said. "I think you could survive on rice and some blankets." At another shelter we met Wolf Cloud, a 24-year-old intermittent southbound through-hiker who considered himself something of a survivalist. "It's just much easier now." He looked at his wool sweater, a throwback. "Fleece is lighter, more comfortable, and it dries a lot faster."

The mechanics of camping ceased to be an issue for Rob and me, too. Now, near the end of a day, we easily identify and agree on a campsite. One fetches water while the other sets up a stove. Tents are up in moments, and we purify water and prepare dinner familiarly and in silence. The silence, in a way, is what we're there for.

They say spring climbs a mountain at about six feet a day, and last week's hike kept us right on the front lines. In protected mountain gaps, Mayapple leaves stretched out like firm, tropical umbrellas; on the ridges, they stayed tightly wrapped around their central stalks, as if for warmth against the still-chilly winds. One morning we got a few flakes of snow. On another, a spring dripping through a mossy rock grotto had created icicles six inches long, while next to the rocks bright yellow trout lilies stretched into the morning sun. Spring, it seemed, was winning.

George Ziegenfuss (Ziggy), 66, a retired minister from western Virginia, was on his second through-hike when we met him the night before we reached Hot Springs. He explained in a soft voice why hikers are so keen to know the names of the Dutchman's-breeches, violets and trilliums they see.

"How many friends do you have whose names you do not know?" he asked, like a Zen master. Say, then, that among our friends this week we counted a barred owl, whose "Who cooks for you?" made us feel safe one night in our tents. We also met a peregrine falcon, a raven and a busy flock of red crossbills, all found south of New England only in the high-

In the raking sunlight of early morning, Harper's Fairy heads north on the trail past a flowering pear tree, through the Mills Ridge area north of Hot Springs, North Carolina. Photo by Rob Cross, News & Observer

er elevations of the Appalachian Mountains.

Hiking among friends may be why we wanted so badly to catch Keebler and Pearl Drops. We were still in high spirits when we reached Max Patch (4,629 feet), a breathtaking mountaintop meadow buffeted by whipping winds. There, on top, we met a day hiker who had been to Hot Springs the day before. He told us that Pearl Drops and Keebler had headed north from town that morning.

So we remained a day or so behind. We'll still try to catch up. Until then we consoled ourselves with the comforts to be found in Hot Springs: a long soak in the rejuvenated spa from which the town got its name, a good meal at the Inn at Hot Springs, a massage and a rest before again setting out north.

▲ Trail Mix—

We've been out long enough to be able to master rudimentary wilderness skills. When we've fallen in behind others we can now tell how far ahead they are and—usually—how many there are by their bootprints. We can also, in a moment, distinguish among the whisper of high wind, the wet hiss of a river, the

The trail is not always a quiet mountain ridge. Interstate construction in Sam's Gap in North Carolina forces the trail to follow the road for a quarter of a mile. Here a speeding truck passes two hikers. Photo by Rob Cross, News & Observer

spatter of raindrops and the angry roar of traffic in a gap. Just two weeks ago, those sounds were an indistinguishable rush. ▲

Signs along the trail keep hikers posted on where they are—and where they might wish to go. Photo by Rob Cross, News & Observer

ERWIN, TENNESSEE

Harper's Fairy snapped her head up from her camp stove, suddenly alert. "Did that sound like a car door?" she asked. Rob and I heard only the spring peepers by the pond near our campsite.

Sure enough, visible through the trees was a silver Mercedes, its driver looking down at the pond. Harper's Fairy kept stirring her tomato-lentil stew. But she didn't relax until we heard another slam and the car's engine start up, then fade as it disappeared down the Forest Service road. For a woman on the Appalachian Trail, that's how it is. "I'm not afraid on the trail," she said, "but I am at road crossings, or at shelters that you could hear a road nearby."

When she's not on the AT, Harper's Fairy is Tracy Brumbaugh, a 29-year-old registered nurse from Hollidaysburg, Pennsylvania. She's hiking for adventure—but she carries pepper spray in her pouch.

"I haven't taken it out," she said, "but I've had it right under the zipper. I don't ignore that feeling."

By not camping near road crossings, trusting her gut feelings about people and simply being sensible, Harper's Fairy is following the advice of every trail agency: Be no less sensible on the trail than you would walking the streets at home.

No, the trail is not perfectly safe. There have been seven murders in the history of the Appalachian Trail, according to Brian King of the Appalachian Trail Conference. There have also been rapes, harassment and

The sun has just risen, and through-hikers (left to right) Berryman Green V (Lonefeather), Roger Contento (Restart), Ben Harth (Kaptain Krumholtz) and Daniel Yoder (Onward) get ready to hit the trail north out of the Jerrys Cabin shelter. Onward is getting water out of a water bag for his breakfast; hikers hang their food to protect it from shelter mice. Photo by Rob Cross, News & Observer

assaults. Portions of the trail in Tennessee, where family squabbles, resentment of hikers and age-old resistance to "the government trail" still exist, have historically been rougher than others.

But King reminds us that, if you multiply the two million hikers who use the trail each year by 58 years of trail use, you get seven murders among more than 100 million people.

▲ **E q u i p m e n t   C h e c k —**
The equipment of the week is Rob's headlamp, a flashlight powered by two AA batteries that he replaces every couple of weeks. I'm clenching a tiny flashlight in my teeth and drooling on my journal, while Rob comfortably writes, cooks, packs and performs any number of camp tasks after dark using two hands. Many hikers have these headlamps, and they love them. I expect this will be my last trip without one. ▲

Still, every hiker at least thinks about safety. At No Business Knob, Jeff Charland (Cruz Control), a 23-year-old social worker from Maine hiking the trail with his dog, Hopalong, described a night when he and a partner heard people in the hollow below shooting guns.

"Our imaginations were going," he said. "We thought they were drunk and shooting all over. You hear, especially from up North, 'Don't go down South! Have you seen 'Deliverance'?'"

But his attitude changed "after five minutes on the trail," he said. "Once [local] people are bending over backwards to help you, it's hard to fear. Now I see an old beat-up pickup and I think, 'Whoa! More colorful characters!'"

We ran into Cruz Control a few times last week, but Harper's Fairy was our companion. We happened upon her at that pond the first night out of Hot Springs. She stayed with us among the rhododendrons on the ridge overlooking Allen Gap. She camped with us on Sugarloaf Knob, where the owls hooted loud enough to keep us awake. And she

It's a strike! Through-hikers Tanner Critz (Wayah, left) and John Bevens (Jones) kill some time after a resupply day in Elk Park, North Carolina, with a little baseball at the Apple House shelter. They made the plate out of a foam sitting pad, the bat out of firewood and the ball out of that most useful of camping items: duct tape. Photo by Rob Cross, News & Observer

Dawn on Big Bald outlines Tracy Brumbaugh (Harper's Fairy), a couple of packs and the signs placing the elevation at 5,516 feet.
Photo by Rob Cross, News & Observer.

pitched her tent with ours on Big Bald (5,516 feet), where we saw a marsh hawk wheel in a 30-mph wind from the treeless summit, then watched the sun sink below the western mountains. We fell asleep beneath the stars, and a few hours later awoke to see the sun turn the sky orange, then appear as a smoky pink disk over the mountains in the east.

She pointed out yellow cinquefoils blooming along the trail, and galaxes, which smell like gas. She spotted snakes and shared Rob's interest in the rufous-sided towhee, which pelted us with its calls of "Drink your TE-EE-EA! Drink your TE-EE-EA!" (Our early-morning response: "Shut your BI-II-ILL!")

Harper's Fairy was part of our team.

Teams are the social fabric of the trail.

An insect crawls across a trillium in bloom along the trail in Tennessee. Photo by Rob Cross, News & Observer.

Most hikers start from Springer Mountain alone, hitching up with others for anywhere from an hour to months. Groups of compatible hikers form, shift, break apart and reform daily on the trail, like cliques at a six-month cocktail party.

At the Jerry Cabin shelter we talked with Roger Contento (Restart), a 53-year-old from Del Mar, New York, who was trying to finish the trail after stopping once before.

"I've been walking with them for about two weeks now," he said of his companions Cruz Control, Little Squaw, Onward, Kaptain Krumholz and Cain. "We just have a good time."

Those who don't work out just speed up or

slow down, and most hikers are wary about sharing their itineraries before they're certain they want another hiker's company.

We're still trying to keep in touch with Keebler and his mom, Pearl Drops. We get messages from them at least twice a week in trail rosters, telling us to hurry up. From Hot Springs, we sent a postcard with our itinerary to what we believe was their next mail drop. We hope we find out this week whether they got it.

The trail this week, more backwoods than wilderness, was perfect for the genial companionship of teams. We passed miles of rusted barbed wire, climbed old logging railroad grades, trudged along dusty roadbeds on sunny days. We crossed highways, peered into slat-sided barns, heard the cackle of chickens and the creaking of farm machinery. The trail has felt like the backyard path you used to take to your best friend's house—behind toolsheds, along untended gardens, through hedges. This week we have felt as if we were behind the garage of Appalachian America. It's not the grandeur of the high Smokies, but it feels comfortable and homely and true.

It was a wonderful walk—wonderful except for the weather. The early April heat has been tremendous—the thermometer at the Erwin Motel read 92 the day we came off the trail. The forest service hasn't yet banned fires, but that may come. We are reassured that it would take months of hot, dry weather to affect the springs we depend on for water, but the storms predicted for this week already seem welcome—a rare sentiment among hikers.

Next week takes us to the last high mountains of the South. As we've gained altitude we seem to have outrun spring, and we're all praying for leaves to protect us from the sun.

Until then, rain will have to do.

▲ Trail Mix—

The term is trail magic, and after you've been on the trail a few weeks, it's everywhere. This week it found An Appalachian Adventure.

Trail magic is anything good or beautiful or marvelous or unexpected that happens on the trail. For us, trail magic started with Harper's Fairy. It's nice that Harper's Fairy is a good hiking companion. But more,

Wilbur, 48, and Reinhold, 19, a father-son team from Massachusetts, cross Yellow Mountain, north of the Overmountain shelter on the North Carolina–Tennessee border. Photo by Rob Cross, News & Observer

It's dinnertime early in the evening, and Fabian Radcliffe (Optimist) prepares the main course while John Knight (Greylag), his hiking partner for decades, enjoys a steaming drink. Camp this evening was in Deep Gap. Photo by Rob Cross, News & Observer

Through-hiker Optimist, a member of the Dominican Order, holds an Easter mass in front of the Apple House shelter. His hiking partner, Greylag, sits to his right. Other through-hikers listening are (from left) Jones, Squirrel Fight, Joker's Wild and Wayah. Photo by Rob Cross, News & Observer

Harper's Fairy is an early riser. Before dawn she boils water for coffee and tea, which she delivers to Rob and me in our sleeping bags.

That's trail magic.

It was trail magic when a friendly native drove us a mile to a spring and back so we could fill our water bags and camp on Big Bald, which has no water. It was trail magic on Big Bald when five cars and trucks drove up full of locals with beer and cigarettes. They stayed for only 15 minutes, all the while telling us local legends and lore. It was trail magic when last week Ziggy spilled his last dehydrated dinner—and Rob had an extra.

Trail magic was stopping at the Country Scrub Board coin laundry in Erwin and having manager Kathy Moore ask if we might like a pepperoni pizza she had ordered, then decided that she didn't want.

Trail magic was Kathy's friend stopping by just as we were finishing our laundry and saying, "I guess you'll be needing a ride to your motel then," and touring us around Erwin's historical train sheds on the way.

Trail magic is a walk down an old

A green snake keeps a watchful eye——and a careful tongue——out to make sure it's not stepped on by hikers. Photo by Rob Cross, News & Observer

Section hiker Terry Jones, from Jonesboro, Tennessee, pours dishwater from the deck of the Overmountain shelter. Photo by Rob Cross, News & Observer

railroad grade along barbed-wire fences. Trail magic is sitting alone by the side of a singing brook after filling my water bottle and getting lost just for a moment in the sun flashing on the ripples. It's the orange, black and brown pebbles below the surface of the creek, the drips off the green moss into a shadowy pool, the progress of silt as it covers a leaf.

Trail magic is why we're here. ▲

DENNIS COVE, TENNESSEE

Looking out at the wrinkled ridges visible from Little Rock Knob (4,919 feet), I got frustrated. Somewhere around there we were supposed to find the oldest rocks on the Appalachian Trail. But which rocks? In the cliffs above and below the trail we recognized striated sandstone and gray shale, but those were deposited only hundreds of millions of years ago. We were looking for rocks, depending on which guidebook we checked, that were between 1.8 and 2.5 billion years old. What we needed was a geologist.

Trail magic being what it is, we found one over the next ridge. And not just any geologist either. We stumbled onto the campsite of Dan Walker, of the North Carolina Geological Survey, hiking a section of the trail. He gave us coffee and Apple Newtons.

"It's called cranberry gneiss [pronounced 'nice']," he said of the base rock described in the guidebooks; he placed it at more like 1.2 billion years old. It was deposited, he said, when what are now the Appalachians were part of a huge, ancient continent.

Mountains are built when continents slam into each other, he told us, and the edge of North America has been slammed into three times in the last 500 million years. The first two times the collision was with Europe, which explains why the mountains of the United Kingdom and Scandinavia resemble the northern Appalachians. The last time, about 250 million years ago, it was Africa that ran into North America, and that created the southern Appalachians.

"But it's all the same stuff," Walker said of the raw materials of the mountains. "It's like a car that's been in multiple wrecks. It just shows the results of the last wreck." Formed through metamorphic processes a billion years ago, the cranberry gneiss has moved around since but has not been transformed.

We think we found some of it. Gray, grainy rock, covered with lichens, it looked right and felt old—whether 1.2 or 2.5 billion years we couldn't say. But as Walker said, geologists have been hanging around the Appalachians for 200 years, and

Spring is making its way north, and this iris is proof. Photo by Rob Cross, News & Observer

Tom Kadamus (Tutone), 24, from Enfield, Connecticut, sleeps the novel way outside the Watauga Lake shelter. Photo by Rob Cross, News & Observer

they still haven't puzzled out all the details.

This was a week of such mysteries for us.

Standing on Hump Mountain (5,587 feet) we were able to do something that's relatively rare in the southern Appalachians: We could see 360 degrees. Tree line in the South is estimated at 7,200 feet, but the summit of Hump is a bald: a windswept, treeless mountain top. We could see Roan Mountain to the south, Grandfather Mountain in North Carolina to the east and ridges stretching away in endless gray rows in every direction. Even on a day so bright that we squinted, the scene was forbidding and awesome.

This week we crossed six balds. Everyone agrees that balds are starkly beautiful, but nobody agrees on how they got that way.

Some hold that they are vestiges of flora that thrived during the last ice age and died off afterward. Cherokee myth says a monster, the Ulagu, used to fly in and carry off their children; after men killed the monster, the balds were created to provide spots to watch from in case another Ulagu came. Others claim that the Cherokee burned the balds to create gamelands.

Early European settlers used the balds for grazing; no longer grazed, they are now being overrun by blackberry bushes and trees. To maintain them, the U.S. Forest Service burns some and is grazing goats on others.

The rain we prayed for last week arrived in torrents on Wednesday, and it rained again as Rob and I came off the trail near Dennis Cove. Just as significant was the wind that followed. It roared for days, during which we always felt as though we were near a waterfall. We had to help each other hold down flapping tent corners.

We noticed this most as we set up camp outside the Overmountain shelter, a charming refurbished barn north of Roan Mountain. Since it already held 14 people, we pitched our tents outside it, on the ridge overlooking the wide valley of the Roaring Creek, and from our tent doors watched a full moon rise over Yellow Mountain.

Keebler, my 12-year-old pal at least a week ahead of us now, got the postcard I sent him from Hot Springs; I also got a phone message at my office from his grandmother. He knows we probably won't catch him, she said, but he's doing fine. He still regularly sends his regards in trail registers.

Spring still shuffles her feet in the mountains; among the few new flowers we saw were trillium, a large red or white beauty with huge green leaves, and squawroot, a hideous oak-root parasite resembles a paleorange pinecone. Other signs of spring have arrived, too. Bees fill cherry trees with droning, and if I turn over rocks when I go

to fill my canteen, I find salamanders.

A few trees have budded: buckeyes, with their five leaves splayed like fingers; hornbeams, whose muscled-looking trunks seem to be clenching to squeeze out their tiny palegreen leaves; and chestnuts, whose damn-the-blight shoots come up year after year from the stumps of their ancestors. When we descended to Dennis Cove we saw, for the first time, more than the occasional smudge of green among the gray trunks.

If the rain forecast to continue this week brings more green, we won't even mind the wind.

▲ Trail Mix —

Shake any through-hiker by the heels and a tiny white piece of quartz will pop out of some pocket; virtually all hikers carry one of the little stones for luck. Geologist Dan Walker explained to us that the quartz is common for two reasons. First, quartz melts at a lower temperature than the surrounding sandstone and other rock do. So when pressure and temperature cause rocks to metamorphose, quartz melts and flows into cracks and crevices. It crystallizes as it cools. In its crystal form it then erodes more slowly than the surrounding rock, so large pieces of quartz are everywhere in the Appalachian Mountains, underfoot to be picked up as lucky stones by hikers. ▲

Perhaps the model backpacker, a turtle makes its weary way up Pond Mountain. Photo by Rob Cross, News & Observer

This wooden sign welcomes hikers to Damascus, Virginia, the "friendliest town on the trail." Photo by Rob Cross, News & Observer

DAMASCUS, VIRGINIA

Ten miles south of Damascus, I resisted sanity.

I had walked 16.2 miles. It was 4 P.M. and I was considering walking the remaining 10 miles into Damascus. Sixteen miles had been my longest day to date, and the prospect of adding 10 more gave me pause.

I was not alone. Law student Nigel Maguire (Sulu), 22, of Fleet, England, had left a half hour before me from the shelter we had shared the night before. I caught up with him at Abingdon Gap, where he and his three companions were trying to decide whether to go on. Sulu was filled with nervous energy while he waited for them to refill their water jugs.

"It's crazy," he said, pacing. "I don't know why we're doing it."

Then the gleam returned to his eyes. "Damascus fever is all I can say," he grinned. "Just get there." He and his companions shouldered their packs and headed north, trying to cram in 26 miles of hiking before the light died.

The backpacking flag is a common sight in Damascus. Sara Rushing (Peppy), Derek Gaasch (Doubletime) and Jessica Clymer (Flower) head for the camping store on Laurel Street, the town's main thoroughfare. Photo by Rob Cross, News & Observer

CHECKLIST

Through-hikers usually go from seven to 10 days between resupply stops in trail towns. When they arrive tired, filthy, hungry and smelly from a week on the trail, they aim to fill several needs, often without staying overnight.

A highly informal poll yielded this ranking of the requirements of a good trail town.

1. Post office. Hikers mail themselves supplies that would be expensive or impossible to obtain in small or isolated towns.

2. Good restaurant, preferably an all-you-can-eat.

3. Shower.

4. Cheap bed for a night or a few nights.

5. A place to do laundry, which smells no better than the hikers.

6. Good market for food resupply.

7. Good outfitter.

8. A cobbler, for resewing or repairing boots and packs.

9. Friendly locals.

A few minutes later, so did I.

That's the pull of the greatest trail town of them all.

Northbound through-hikers have been anticipating Damascus for weeks now. Some 451.4 miles north of Springer Mountain, Georgia, it's a fifth of the way through the trail. In Damascus, known as "the friendliest town on the trail," hikers get more than food and rest.

"It's the first milestone for a through-hiker to hit," said Tom Kadamus (Tutone), 24, a recent college graduate from Enfield, Connecticut, who along with his boyhood pal Mark Moody (Chippy), 22, of Lincoln, Maine had spent a night with us at the Watauga Lake shelter two nights before. There, almost 40 miles south of Damascus, they grew excited. "We'll get there in two days," Tutone said, stretching the hikers' average of 14 miles a day.

The trail this week was remarkably flat. We climbed Iron Mountain (4,120 feet), crossed to Holston Mountain (about 4,100 feet), then for some 30 miles never climbed or descended more than about 400 feet. But it wasn't easy walking that drove Tutone and Chippy. It was Damascus fever.

For Rob and me, the week didn't start with Damascus fever. It started with the gorge

His own shadow is all the company that photographer Rob Cross has one early morning near Buzzard Rock (about 5,000 feet) in Virginia. The mountain in the background is Beech Mountain (4,766). Not far from here Cross got some company—a brief visit from a bear. Photo by Rob Cross, News & Observer

where the Laurel Fork spills down a 40-foot cascade through sheer cliffs into a deep, cold pool. It wasn't quite warm enough for swimming, but we soaked our feet. We pitched our tents that night a mile south, in pine straw surrounded by hemlocks and rhododendrons. The river burbled us to sleep.

The next day our walk to the Watauga Lake shelter where we met Tutone and Chippy was easy. Talking to them the following night inspired us to walk 13 miles instead of our scheduled 10. After that, at the Iron Mountain shelter, we met Sulu and his friends Sara Rushing (Peppy), Rebecca Ard (Sunshine) and Jeff Tober (Father Time), students in their early 20s.

Their easy intimacy as they lit their gas stoves and spread their gear around the shelter reminded us of our own companions of recent

weeks. At Damascus, since hikers often stay for several days instead of only one, through-hikers bunch up, which permits them to catch up with other hikers they may have lost track of.

The next morning, Sulu and his friends conferred in hushed tones, then shared with us their plan to proceed. They were giddy.

Rob, a sane soul, never considered 26.2 miles—the distance of a marathon—with 50 pounds strapped to his back. We had traveled 8 easy miles by 10:30 A.M. and stopped for lunch at a shelter. In the register there, I found a week-old note from Keebler, crowing about going 19.2 miles one day.

I caught the fever; I could barely stand still long enough to wish Rob a pleasant two days on the trail.

I was going in.

My senses worked as swiftly as my legs;

the pace didn't cloud my perception. Looking over the green ridges, I felt as though my eyes were taking clear, permanent snapshots. I especially remember a view south from the Holston Ridge into Shady Valley, Tennessee. It had rained the night before, and as I surveyed the pale- and deep-green squares of fields in the sun-dappled valley, for the first time on the trip I thought of the word "lush." Wisps of fog floated in hollows, and far below I could see trucks and silos.

More rain and milder temperatures this week have coaxed leaves from the trees; soon we would be walking in a green forest.

But that day, I was just concentrating on walking 26 miles—or trying to. I don't think I actually expected to make Damascus until I rounded a bend and saw Sulu and his friends scarfing the last food from their packs. Peppy, 22, from Cincinnati demanded that, exhausted as we were, we walk into town as a group. The setting sun slanted through hemlocks as we descended the last 2 miles to town.

Suddenly, Sunshine, 21, from Traverse City, Michigan broke into a grin. "Listen!" she said. "First you hear the cars, then the dogs barking. Then lawn mowers, then the voices."

With water steaming for morning coffee right outside the door, Scott Huler's tent forms the perfect frame for the sunrise over White-top Mountain in Virginia. Photo by Scott Huler, News & Observer

A leucothoe blooms along the trail in Virginia. Photo by Rob Cross, News & Observer

We descended past rooftops, lawns and, finally, kids on bicycles. People waved at us and shouted greetings. Damascus deserves its reputation, with "Welcome hikers" signs in every window and hiker registers in most of the stores. The Laundromat was closed, and the barking dogs seemed mean; otherwise it was perfect.

My 26-mile day was a success. I reached Damascus in time to catch John Knight (Greylag) and Fabian Radcliffe (Optimist), two sixtyish British gentlemen whom we had met the week before. The next morning, we shared a wonderful breakfast at Dot's, a place of worn wooden floors, ceiling fans and orange Formica tables.

I had lunch with college student Tanner Critz (Wayah). "There's that one-day overlap," he said. "Suddenly, everybody knows where everybody is. It's cool." Rob arrived the next day, and we caught up with Harper's Fairy, with whom we had hiked for two weeks, and, predictably, with Tutone and his gang.

For the hikers, Damascus feels like high school on Friday night. Hikers drift from hos-tel to restaurant to store, talking, hugging and relaxing. At night they go to Dot's and with the locals form an easy, smiling group.

But it can't last.

On Monday morning Sulu, Tutone and their companions, along with friends who are not yet ready to leave, filled three booths at Dot's, pouring quarters into the jukebox and dawdling over coffee.

It was time to go. Dot's grew quiet, like a locker room before game time. Velcro ripped, zippers buzzed, snaps snapped. Hugs were exchanged, promises made.

And then, loosely together, the hikers filed out. Sixteen miles up the trail, they would convene at a shelter.

Dot's—and Damascus—would fill up with the next group.

▲ Trail Mix—

We ran into a lot of old friends in Damascus, but the best surprise came after we bumped into our old friend Ben Carey (Sparrow Hawk), 20, of Bethlehem, Connecticut. We remember him from our start at Springer Mountain, Georgia. We only caught up with him because he spent a week off the trail with shin splints. He was 50 miles behind his trail friends, but they were coming to pick him up at The Place, a rooming facility run by the local Methodist church.

We stuck around to see his friends, and when Pearl Drops and Keebler got out of the car to pick him up, they

seemed as delighted to see us as we were to see them. Keebler misses his friends from home, but he's having a great time with Sparrow Hawk. ▲

ATKINS, VIRGINIA

Bojo looked at me with a great weariness. The 40-year-old from Bangor, Maine left Mount Katahdin in October and has been walking south ever since. In 1991 he through-hiked the Appalachian Trail. Hiking north that time, he had plenty of company.

This time he started alone, southbound. Seven months later he's three-quarters of the way through, but with none of the north-bounders' camaraderie.

"I'm more like the stranger passing by," he said. He nodded and then, alone, walked on.

Sam Lockhart, (Sam I Am) of Meeker, Colorado, crosses a rolling Virginia meadow. Photo by Rob Cross, News & Observer

Outside the O'Lystery Community Picnic shelter, through-hiker Jim Hall (Jungle Jim), of Massachusetts, savors a smoke while checking out the next day's hike north. Photo by Rob Cross, News & Observer

I walked on alone, too.

After five weeks in the company of other hikers, photographer Rob Cross and I spent a week apart, avoiding even each other, seeking solitude.

We found it largely by skipping the shelters. I camped alone every night all week; I never saw more than three people during any one day. When you don't go looking for people, you don't find them.

We crossed territory that was perfect for solitary walking. We climbed Whitetop Mountain, Virginia's second-highest peak at 5,520

feet and a breathtaking bald nestled against 5,729-foot Mount Rogers. The latter is the highest point in the state and the last peak above 5,000 feet that hikers will encounter until they reach New Hampshire. Shrouded in a spruce-fir forest, Mount Rogers, which hikers reach by a short side trail, was so cool that its mossy shadows still held snow from a storm we missed by two days.

The highlight of the week, though, was the Grayson Highlands, a 4,000-foot-high, 4,700-acre region of rolling meadows studded with huge cliffs of 500-million-year-old volcanic rhyolite. Wild ponies roam the grassy terrain, which is broken only by groves of rhododendrons, azaleas and occasional apple trees. It's a magnificent, desolate walk, one that northbound hikers commonly call the most beautiful on the trail up to that point.

It was especially stirring seen alone. The wind whipping across the ridges made the cliffs seem big and unforgiving. The sun disappearing behind one of the puffy white clouds was enough to make me fiercely aware of my solitude, its return enough to make me suddenly exult.

"You have to be with yourself and reflect on yourself," Bojo had said of walking alone. "You probably see a little more of yourself than you'd like." Like so many hikers on the trail, I was fresh off a significant change in my life—the end of my marriage—so I expected the self-examination.

What I didn't expect was how quickly that self-examination passed. The first lesson of the trail, hikers tell each other, is to hike your own hike: Control only what you can, and let the trail do the rest. I sang aloud, talked to myself and engaged in screaming arguments with associates past and present, but the trail quickly rendered those disputes irrelevant. I was carrying all the food and clothing I needed. My only concerns were water and a flat place to camp. That simplification was wonderfully clarifying.

Nobody walking alone considers himself to be self-sufficient; loneliness prevents that.

▲ Equipment Check—
Equipment Check. When we camp together, Rob calls my cylindrical aluminum candle lamp my porch light, because I like to hang it above my tent door. "I can tell you're at home," he says. Every night this week the candle provided my solitary camps with a pleasing light at dusk and, behind the safety of its glass cover, a little flame. Almost like a fireplace, the lantern warmed the tent on chilly nights. Every night it warmed my heart when I lit it for comfort. As Rob said, it meant I was home. ▲

Rhododendrons line the trail for thousands of miles. It was indisputably spring when this one bloomed. Photo by Rob Cross, News & Observer

Self-reliance, though, I found.

With my time filled by the minutiae of camping, my days found a rhythm. Mornings became a ritual. I woke with the lightening of the sky. Thanks to my little butane stove stowed at the door of my tent, I had water for coffee and oatmeal boiling moments later. A three-minute emergence to get my food and use the woods, and I was back in my sleeping bag for a 10-minute breakfast in bed. After breakfast, I had camp clear in an hour. I hit

A junco at the Cosby Knob shelter. The junco is one of the most common birds along the trail. Photo by Rob Cross, News & Observer

the trail by 8 A.M., far earlier than I did when I walked with others.

Late every afternoon I consulted map and guidebook for a campsite. Around 6, a spot said "home," and I dropped my pack. Fetching and purifying water provided rest, and I could set up my tent in exactly the time it took

water to boil for dinner. Dinner was quiet—I heard deer and birds. Without Rob to identify the birds, I merely listened. Less than an hour after making camp the food was hung for the night, my gear stowed. I usually savored a peaceful hour doing nothing more than sitting quietly, sometimes by a creek, sometimes in a stand of pines, sometimes just in camp. As the week went on, I spent less and less time thinking and more time simply perceiving.

I remember the smell of a dirt road as it absorbed the fat drops of a brief shower, the sound one night of spring peepers that told me of a pond I found the next morning.

One afternoon I crossed a broad meadow to a worn wooden stile. I sat on the top rung, looking out over the farmhouse and fields, and watched the dust raised by a mail car settle. I listened to the wind in the white pines and the tulip poplars, and I felt the hairs on my arm rise in the kind of spring breeze that makes you thank God you have the skin to feel it with.

Bojo said people come out to the woods to find themselves, and don't always like what they find. I was lucky enough, for moments at a time, to lose myself; that seemed even more precious.

My life became elemental: When strong, I walked; when hungry, I ate; when lonely, I cried.

But even the stillness of non-thinking wears thin after a while; I was glad when Rob caught up to me as we walked to our last shelter. There, as we considered dinner, we heard laughter ringing from the hills; we smiled as three convivial hikers arrived.

Michael Denis (Hermit), 22, from Keene, New Hampshire, said he often walked for days on his own but was always glad to meet other hikers, such as his two companions. He said he had more highs and lows when he walked alone. "More so, definitely, than when you're with people. I kind of wanted those. I wanted to sort things out."

He smiled, water coming to a boil in his little pot for a dehydrated dinner. He surveyed the pots and pans spread over the table.

"I sorted them out. Now it's cool to be with people."

I looked around the shelter, filled with food and fuel and guidebooks, and with laughter and conversation.

And I agreed with Hermit.

It was cool to be with people.

▲ **Trail Mix—**
We went through Deep Gap this week; it seems as if we go through a Deep Gap once a week. Buzzsaw—24-year-old Jim Bishop, a teacher from Maine whom we met briefly in Hot Springs—has kept us entertained with his witty register comments since then, and on place names had this to offer: "Ever notice that every place we've been so far on the trail has been some combination of the following 12 words: fork, deep, bald, horse, spring, gap, hog, rocky, creek, knob, big and cow? Just mix and match...Horse Gap, Big Spring ...." Buzzsaw has achieved a level of trail awareness to which we can only aspire. ▲

Toll of the trail

How do eight weeks of hiking affect the human body? Prior to setting out on the Appalachian Trail, reporter Scott Huler, 35, dropped by the Raleigh Athletic Club to have some vital statistics recorded. Then, within a week after completing his 410-mile stint, Huler, who is 6'3", was re-examined. Some key findings:

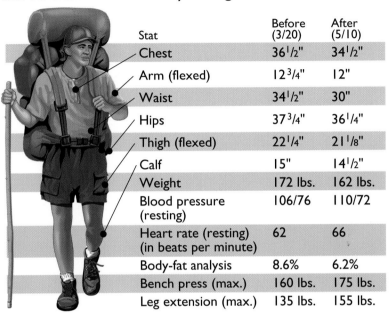

Stat	Before (3/20)	After (5/10)
Chest	36½"	34½"
Arm (flexed)	12¾"	12"
Waist	34½"	30"
Hips	37¾"	36¼"
Thigh (flexed)	22¼"	21⅛"
Calf	15"	14½"
Weight	172 lbs.	162 lbs.
Blood pressure (resting)	106/76	110/72
Heart rate (resting) (in beats per minute)	62	66
Body-fat analysis	8.6%	6.2%
Bench press (max.)	160 lbs.	175 lbs.
Leg extension (max.)	135 lbs.	155 lbs.

Trail diet
An average day of food consumption for a hiker looks something like this:

Food	Calories	Calories from fat	Protein (grams)	Carbohydrates (grams)	Fat (grams)
BREAKFAST					
Oatmeal	160	16	4	33	2
Tangerine	65	0	1	16	0
Pop-Tart	210	70	3	34	7
LUNCH					
Cheese	300	210	21	3	24
Bread	140	5	6	31	0.5
Peanut butter	380	260	16	14	32
Jelly	50	0	0	0	0
Dried-meat stick	280	110	7	0	12
SNACKS					
Snickers bars (2)	560	240	8	72	28
Gorp*	1,240	320	30	174	49
DINNER					
Freeze-dried Lipton dinner	500	60	20	80	8
Total	**3,885**	**1,291**	**116**	**457**	**162.5**

* Includes raisins, peanuts, M&Ms and granola

The U.S. Department of Health and Human Services recommends a normal daily diet of about 2,000 calories.

A person Huler's size, carrying his backpack, walking 3 mph, would burn about 354 calories per hour. By comparison, he might expect to burn 432 calories per hour doing calisthenics or 630 calories per hour swimming.

BLAND, VIRGINIA

As the sun burned off the late morning haze, I sat down to remove my rain parka.

The trail led between rolling hills. A farmhouse sat, white and neat, a quarter of a mile away. I could hear not only cows but roosters and the squawk of a rusty gate. Weathered posts supporting new barbed wire cast abbreviated shadows, as did the dandelions, both yellow tops and white puffs. Blackbirds yelled their heads off in trees filled with pale-green leaves. I couldn't think of a single reason to move. So I sat in the meadow and waited for Rob to catch up.

And I waited. And waited.

I waited nearly a half hour. When he showed up, he told me about a beaver he had been watching. But when he started hobbling behind me, I suspected that there was another reason behind his delay. Rob's knee was giving out.

Henry Tanner (Screaming Coyote), 21, of Raleigh, North Carolina, crosses a stile at VA-610. Coyote is recovering from a stroke, but he gets over the stiles — used to prevent damage to fences at crossings — as well as any other hiker. Photo by Rob Cross, News & Observer

You can't escape your body. It seemed as if half the people we met this week had said goodbye to companions who had been forced off the trail. But for those who were still hiking, six or eight weeks into the trail, physical issues are disappearing. Scott Riddell (Dr. Dooriddell), 32, from Bar Harbor, Maine, announced at the pavilion that he had just finished his first day without moleskin to protect against blisters. Not only that, but he finally felt in shape.

"It's really within the last 10 days or so," he said. "The first four weeks I was hurting every night. Now I'm just stronger. I'm putting in solid days every day. Fourteen to 18 miles seems to be pretty normal."

That makes sense to Dr. Thomas Best, a family and sports-medicine physician at the University of North Carolina at Chapel Hill Medical Center. Through-hikers' bodies, he said, are going through remarkable transformations. "You get a chronic adaptation after about six weeks."

In the first week of hiking, Best said, hikers' bodies produce more red blood cells. This not only gets more oxygen to their muscles but also improves respiration.

But hikers don't experience the most significant breakthrough until about six weeks into their hike, when their bodies have produced more plasma—literally increasing their blood supply—and created more capillaries to carry these blood cells. At the same time, fooled by the backpack into thinking they suddenly weigh 40 to 50 pounds more than they used to, their bodies have increased bone mass in their legs. So hikers' entire bodies are now simply better equipped than before.

Both men and women are susceptible to dehydration and weight loss as their metabolism increases during the hike, but men are much more profoundly affected. Most male through-hikers have lost between 10 and 30

A red columbine makes a comfortable home for a bug along the trail above Laurel Creek. Photo by Rob Cross, News & Observer

pounds after six or eight weeks on the trail, whereas women have tended to gain a few pounds, or at least to lose far less weight. Men's bodies quickly burn fat deposits, leaving the familiar bandy-legged, starved-looking male through-hikers. Women's bodies, Best said, are always hedging against the possibility of pregnancy, so they hormonally reduce metabolism rather than burning fat. Add bone and muscle mass, and you have a stronger, but not much lighter female through-hiker.

Screaming Coyote cooks his dinner outside his tent at the O'Lystery Community Picnic shelter. Photo by Rob Cross, News & Observer

But not every physical change hikers face is related to the trail. We were caught last week by Henry Tanner (Screaming Coyote), 21, a college student from Raleigh, North Carolina, whom we first met near Springer Mountain, Georgia.

Then, he was taking things a week at a time. That hasn't changed. But now he's walked 550 miles—more than a quarter of the Appalachian Trail—and he's recovering from the stroke he suffered exactly a year before starting his hike.

Screaming Coyote wobbles a little, urging his left side along with every step, but he smiles. "There's a lot more rhythm in my walk," he said. "Before, I was falling 15 times a day. Now it's like once or twice when I'm tired. Even my toes are starting to come back to life." Prior to setting out, Screaming

Coyote thought for a long time about what the trail would mean for his recovery. He prepared himself mentally and physically, and through-hikers agree that preparation makes a successful hike.

My last night in a shelter, with Screaming Coyote and Terry Reed (Trekker), 53, from Ocala, Florida was in the huge shelter atop Chestnut Knob, at 4,409 feet the highest through-hikers will get until Mount Moosilauke in New Hampshire.

The Chestnut Knob shelter had windows and a door, which made it delightfully dry as we heard a roaring wind drive rain against the snug roof. From there the week brought more meadows, some filled with grazing cows—a firm stare will move a cow from the trail—and a final long ridge walk into Bland.

Every tree isn't filled, but the leaves are out now. Some rhododendrons and azaleas have bloomed, and we saw columbines. Best, though, were the returning birds. From a campsite overlooking Burke's Garden, a beautiful bowl filled with fertile farmlands, Rob and I saw a scarlet tanager, an indigo bunting, a goldfinch and a blue jay. The gaudy colors reminded us of watching the faculty procession at a college graduation.

▲ **Trail Mix—**
One of the tiny but important questions people asked us at the outset of this project involved pronunciation. And after seeing local television ads every week in motels all the way from Fontana, North Carolina, to Bland, Virginia, we can report that the name starts changing from App-a-LATCH-ians to App-a-LAY-chians somewhere around Atkins, Virginia. ▲

Jack Lundgard (Eagle 1), 60, crosses the Laurel Creek bridge, constructed in 1993 with only traditional tools. Eagle 1 recently lost his wife of 37 years to cancer. Before her death, he said, "she made me promise to hike the trail. And she told me that when I saw butterflies, flowers and birds, that would be her." A tiger swallowtail fluttered by as he wiped away a tear. "There goes my wife again," he said.
Photo by Rob Cross, News & Observer

Atop 3,020-foot Cove Mountain, a short side trail leads to the monolith Dragons Tooth, where Paige Braddock (left) and John Harmon test their climbing skills. Photo by David Tulis, Atlanta Journal-Constitution

SOLACE BUT NO SANCTUARY

M A Y   6 – 2 9 ,   1 9 9 5

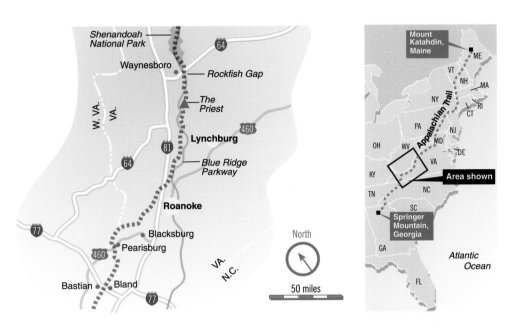

NEWPORT, VIRGINIA

Text and photography by John Harmon

Illustrations by Paige Braddock

Keith Dailey has got this backpacking thing down pat. Known on the trail as Smooth, the 36-year-old former marine from Glengary, West Virginia, carries a pack that usually weighs no more than 30 pounds, walks 20 miles a day, gobbles bacon cheeseburgers whenever he can and loves every minute of it.

Back home, things aren't so smooth. His father needs heart surgery, and his mother has multiple sclerosis and cannot care for herself. Smooth plans to leave the trail soon to help his family, not knowing if he will be able to return in time to reach Maine by winter.

Hikers record their progress, trade gossip and share jokes via shelter logbooks. The register at Jenny Knob Shelter in southwestern Virginia shows one of the many cartoons that Keith Dailey (Smooth) uses to chart his journey. Photo by John Harmon, Atlanta Journal-Constitution

TOP: *The slopes of Brushy Mountain offer a view of Kimberling Creek Valley.* Photo by John Harmon, Atlanta Journal-Constitution

LEFT: *"I cook about five biscuits per person, and there are never any left," says Tillie Wood, who opens her log bunkhouse near Pearisburg, Virginia, to hikers in May and June each year. The first eight risers get a breakfast of sausage, scrambled eggs, biscuits, grits, coffee and orange juice.* Photo by Louie Favorite, Atlanta Journal-Constitution

A native azalea adorns Brushy Mountain. Photo by John Harmon, Atlanta Journal-Constitution

century log barn and feasted on breakfast, a bargain at $3.50.

The first 90 miles of my hike took me through terrain that varied from craggy ridge tops roamed by bears (three adults, including a mother with two cubs, scrambled across my path) to pastoral valleys with whitewashed churches. Through this part of Virginia the trail is surprisingly tough, making steep climbs out of eight valleys to the crests of wind-swept mountains.

One of the most beautiful of these ascents is up Dismal Creek, where I climbed on a sunny morning past waterfalls and weekend campers to stream banks laced with pink and

"I've dreamed of hiking the trail for a long time, but it looks as if I'll have to put it on hold," Smooth says. "That's reality." And reality doesn't stop just because hikers pull on a pack and stride away from their everyday life.

Many view the Appalachian Trail as a 2,100-mile belt of wilderness somehow detached from the real world, a place to be purified by simple thoughts of nature and the fellowship of others who enjoy the same. Perhaps what is most remarkable is how often this vision holds true. As I began my stint on the trail a week ago in Bland, Virginia, my thoughts returned to the six months in 1979 when I through-hiked the Appalachian Trail. I overcame the bites of reality (little money, knee and ankle injuries), while finding the goodness of the trail in the many people who helped along the way.

That giving spirit is still alive in people like Tillie Wood of Roswell, Georgia, who offers hikers a cheap country breakfast and a free place to sleep at Woodshole, her summer retreat near Pearisburg, Virginia. Two other hikers and I slept in her cozy, restored 19th-

As hikers cross the Valley of Virginia, stiles give a boost in scaling pasture fences. Illustration by Paige Braddock, Atlanta Journal-Constitution

white wild azaleas. The trail up Dismal leads past the Wapiti shelter, the place where the trail lost its innocence in 1981.

Two hikers were killed there, their bodies concealed nearby and ashes scattered across the board floor to conceal the bloodstains. It took a few days to discover their bodies, a few weeks to find their killer, now imprisoned. In the intervening weeks, panic dogged the steps of hikers in central Virginia. Many chose to bypass that section of the trail until the killer was arrested. A motive for the killings was never revealed.

Wapiti's troubles weren't over, though. In 1993, a hiker contracted hantavirus, an often fatal infection spread by rodents. Health authorities believe he was exposed to it at

Wapiti or another nearby shelter, although mice trapped in the log shelter tested negative for the virus. The man, who began showing symptoms of fever, chills, nausea and vomiting when he reached Pennsylvania, was hospitalized for four weeks before returning to the trail to finish his through-hike.

Mice in shelters, an annoyance for years, have become an increasing concern in recent years because of hantavirus. To prevent its spread, the Appalachian Trail Conference recommends that hikers store food away from mice, avoid stirring up the dust of mice nests and use a ground cloth to sleep on, rather than resting directly on the shelter floor. I prefer to sleep in a tent; it's cleaner. But many hikers opt for the ready-made shelters.

A fisherman tries his luck at Dismal Falls, along creek banks lined with wild azaleas. Photo by John Harmon, Atlanta Journal-Constitution

A quick stop at Wapiti satisfied my curiosity and I moved on, not wanting to stay even long enough to eat lunch.

By the next day, the rigors of the first week on the trail had taken their toll. I was nursing sore knees as I took careful steps down the steep north slope of Angels Rest. An explosion of wildflowers blooming on the forest floor soon soothed my pain. Solomon's seal, wild geraniums, star chickweed and numerous others washed the mountain in white, purple, yellow and pink.

At 3,800 feet, Angels Rest offers a commanding view into Pearisburg, a way station for backpackers eager for hot showers and clean clothes. From the mountaintop, the red roof of the Pizza Hut shines like a beacon to hungry hikers.

It's a long, hot climb out of the New River Valley at Pearisburg to the top of Peters Mountain. My efforts were rewarded with something few hikers ever see: black bears, five within a 4-mile stretch.

Despite their size—adult males can weigh more than 400 pounds—bears want to avoid contact with humans. The first two encounters were over almost before they happened.

All I saw was a black flash of fur streaking off the trail and down the mountain, sounding like a 1958 Buick rolling through the woods. It was nearing sunset when I spotted the third bear, which hesitated before running downhill out of sight.

Then I saw why she was reluctant to leave. Up the trunk of a tall oak, two cubs quickly climbed, stopping when they neared the top to peer down at me.

Excitedly, I whipped out my camera for a few photographs. About 60 seconds elapsed before I heard the rustling of the underbrush as Mama headed back uphill. I shouldered

Bob Yates (San Diego Bob) crosses the Johns Creek footbridge. Photo by John Harmon, Atlanta Journal-Constitution

my backpack, stepping quickly down the trail, and left Mama to her duties.

Once atop Peters Mountain, I made camp, spending a restless night under a tarp that shook from wind and rain. As the fog lifted from the bald in the early morning, Bob Yates, 48, strode into view, painfully slow but steady through the wet grass.

Writer and photographer John Harmon rests for a while atop the cliffs of Tinker Mountain Photo by David Tulis, Atlanta Journal-Constitution

Since he was the first hiker I met who matched my 12-mile-a-day pace (a more common distance for through-hikers at this point is 15 to 20 miles), we saw much of each other over the next three days, walking through woods abloom with dogwoods and occasionally apple trees from a long-abandoned orchard or homestead.

Eight months ago his wife of 18 years, Mary, died after a five-year fight against brain cancer. Bob (San Diego Bob) decided to escape to the trail.

"I need time to think," he said while eating a supper of some freeze-dried concoction, washed down with Kool-Aid that dripped red in his grayish-blond beard. "And God knows you can talk to yourself for hours out here. By the time I'm finished, I hope to be able to decide what I'm going to do with the rest of my life."

Two weeks ago reality took another bite,

Clinton Boyd fires up his stove at the Lamberts Meadow shelter. Photo by David Tulis, Atlanta Journal-Constitution

when Bob sprained his left ankle. It's black and blue and still swollen, but he plods along gingerly, stubbornly refusing to quit.

BIG ISLAND, VIRGINIA

If backpacking is my church, I now understand that the Appalachian Trail is my high cathedral.

The last 17 days on the trail have been like a homecoming, the longest walk I have taken on this footpath since I through-hiked it in 1979. For 188 miles I have walked, climbed and sometimes stumbled across the mountains of central Virginia, finding a trail that has changed yet, for me, remains much the same.

Here, the trail is better maintained and almost fully protected from the development that was smothering it 16 years ago. Some stretches have been relocated miles away, to

On Apple Orchard Mountain, a clump of rare yellow lady's slippers brightens the trail. Photo by John Harmon, Atlanta Journal-Constitution

From atop the half-mile-long Tinker Cliffs, hikers catch a glimpse of Catawba Valley in Virginia. Photo by David Tulis, Atlanta Journal-Constitution

government-owned land cocooned from development. The most noticeable difference, though, is the hikers themselves: Far more are middle-aged and older, reflecting the increase in baby boomers who want to keep on trekking and senior citizens who in retirement find the time to realize a dream.

Unchanged is the spirit of the trail, which makes the Appalachian Trail more than just a footpath along the knobby spine of eastern America. It is the place where I have learned patience by pacing myself up hills, kindness from strangers who helped along the way, tenacity from refusing to quit even when I

hurt and courage from seeing others overcome personal obstacles.

It seems that good things happen on the trail, even when they come disguised.

Seven months ago, during a weekend backpacking trip to train for this hike, I awoke with pains knifing my right side. The next morning brought the most difficult walk I've ever faced on the Appalachian Trail—the 4 miles to the car that would take me to a North Carolina hospital where my appendix was removed.

Follow-up tests revealed an early-stage, cancerous tumor in one kidney. A few weeks later, in December, my right kidney was removed. I was left with a 12-inch-long scar in my side but a good prognosis, since the appendicitis led doctors to discover the tumor before it spread.

"You know what I'm thinking about?" I murmured the next day to my wife, Lisa, as she sat at my side. "I'm thinking about being back on the Appalachian Trail next May."

Life is so beautiful and then you have cancer. It's a disease that forces you to confront fears of dying, and I was helped through it by knowing the trail was waiting. Death seems far less terrifying when you're walking in the woods.

Back in the 1970s, the hikers I met spent little time discussing the spiritual nature of the trail. Maybe it was because we were mostly college kids so wrapped up in our adventure that it was nearly over before its deeper aspects touched us. Today seems little different: As northbound through-hikers in Virginia pass the 600-mile mark, the trail registers remain full of chat about food in the next town or teasing about how fast or slow some backpacker is.

At 40 I have other concerns, and so do many of the hikers in their middle years and beyond.

"We older guys hike slow enough to smell the flowers," explains Robert Shedd, 73, of Voorheesville, New York, a retired carpenter who has been hiking sections of the Appalachian Trail since 1991. Jack Lundgard, 60, sets a faster pace. The Panama City, Florida, man walks 15 or 20 miles daily. Regardless of pace, many of the older hikers I met can relate to the spirit of the trail.

Dave Tulis and I had covered an exhausting day of 14 miles when we finally stomped

Rocky road: Bud Braddock takes a break. Illustration by Paige Braddock, Atlanta Journal-Constitution

Virginia Tech student Ulla Reeves relaxes at the base of Dragons Tooth with Ty, at her feet, and Cisero. Photo by David Tulis, Atlanta Journal-Constitution

down into the hollow of the Lamberts Meadow shelter, swarming with stinging gnats. That day we had hiked along the spectacular cliffs of McAfee Knob and Tinker Mountain, with views into valleys checkered with newly plowed fields.

Lundgard, a retired Air Force colonel who hikes with the name Eagle 1, met us at the shelter. To help with arthritic knees, he uses lightweight aluminum hiking poles in each hand.

His wife died of cancer last year. She had gotten sick for the last time in 1993, forcing him off the trail in Pennsylvania about 1,000 miles from his goal. He is hiking the whole trail this year, in part, he says, to be with her.

"Before she died, my wife told me to go back and finish the trail," he told us, tears welling in his eyes. "She told me that she would be the butterflies, the birds and the flowers. So every time I see a butterfly, I say 'Hi, sweetie.'"

The next few days, the path led us from the

Allegheny Mountains and their long, rocky ridges across the Valley of Virginia, with its abandoned apple orchards overgrown with flowering white roses and the drone of traffic on I-81, and up into the rumpled Blue Ridge Mountains. As we neared the Blue Ridge Parkway, the trail often tunneled through rhododendron thickets heavy with purple flowers.

I ended an afternoon of rambling through this lovely garden at the Wilson Creek shelter, where I shared a campsite with a backpacker who perhaps best summed up what the trail means to so many. Jean Hermasen, 56, has covered all but 300 miles of the Appalachian Trail in sections since 1992. She had to postpone such adventures until her five children were grown, though two are in junior college and still live at home.

"There's nothing between you and God out here," she said, the morning sun sparkling on her gray hair. "You can't help but talk to God if you stay out long enough."

Hung out to dry: At the Punchbowl shelter, on the shore of a pond, it's time to come clean. Photo by David Tulis, Atlanta Journal-Constitution

Rhododendron tunnels, such as this one near Rice Mountain, Virginia, are a common sight along the trail in the South. Hikers walk beneath the arching branches. Photo by David Tulis, Atlanta Journal-Constitution

LEFT: *Lisa (left) and Martha Ezzard take a trail-mix break after the 3,000-foot climb to the summit of Bald Knob.* Photo by David Tulis, Atlanta Journal-Constitution

BELOW: *The Pedlar Dam spillway cascades past hikers along the trail. The spillway stands 75 feet tall and 435 feet wide, holding back 82 million gallons of water in Pedlar Lake, the drinking water supply for the city of Lynchburg, Virginia.* Photo by David Tulis, Atlanta Journal-Constitution

ROCKFISH GAP, VIRGINIA

Text by Martha Ezzard

"Maps are a male thing," teased my daughter as the two of us wiped away the sweat with red bandannas. Lisa pored over the map I'd so carelessly neglected to check after crossing the James River. Admittedly, a

trailhead sign was missing, but that was no excuse for my failure to look for white blazes as we hiked nearly 2.5 miles off course.

Lisa and I had entered the George Washington National Forest before noon, talking not about maps and miles but about Yankee birds and Southern gentlemen.

The songbird tape we'd been listening to during our drive to Lynchburg told us an astonishing thing: Birds have Southern accents, too—regional differences in song just from frequenting the same habitat. We detected the "teakettle, teakettle" tune of a Carolina wren right off—not bad for amateur birders. Unlike the wren, though, 75 percent of Virginia's songbirds are migratory. They have been dwindling in numbers since the late '60s, as their summertime old-growth habitat on the East Coast has dwindled along with their winter habitat in shrinking forest tracts in South America.

A lady's slipper grows trailside. Illustration by Paige Braddock, Atlanta Journal-Constitution

As for Southern gentlemen, Pedlar District Chief Forester James Hunt surely qualified. Not only had he shuttled us to the trail, but he also suggested gently that he'd be happy to mail back anything we wanted to dump to lighten our load. We laughed. Our chief aim had been to keep our packs under 35 pounds. Extra apples and face cream were gone, and we were gladly cramming ourselves into a smaller tent because it weighed only three pounds.

Never anticipating how precariously our day would end, I thought its beginning perfect. I had my 31-year-old daughter all to myself, and her reactions to the trail's spring wonders were far more exquisite than mine. Lisa Ezzard, a poet and teacher who lives in California, compared the swirl-like laurel

buds to cake icing and the spider lines inside a blossom to a daddy longlegs. No wonder white blazes weren't on my mind.

By the time we discovered our wrong turn and retraced our steps, we were three hours behind schedule. The next water source and possible campsite were 8 steep miles away.

As the sun began to set, we hit the steepest portion of Three Sisters, the final ascent to Rocky Row. While I struggled for breath, my daughter pulled a role reversal, nurturing me to the top. It was almost 9 P.M. when we reached the sign to Salt Log Gap camp; we had put in a nine-hour, 13-mile day. Our mouths felt like cotton, and there was just a half cup of water between us. We started down an overgrown side trail to the nearest water site, another mile, but it was too dark to see. So we shared our last apple, savoring its juice, saved a few sips of water for morning and fell into our sleeping bags, giggling nervously over our ridiculous start.

The tromping sound of a big animal awoke us at 2 A.M. A deer, we said to each other. But we heard a heavy breathing noise. I rattled a stick and flicked on the flashlight. The tromping faded and returned, then faded again. Lisa slapped her leg and laughed hysterically. "Mom on bear watch," she said. "It doesn't give me confidence."

We found water the next morning and scurried over Bluff Mountain to the Punchbowl shelter, where we rejoined Dave Tulis, who was on the verge of calling the Forest Service to search for us. Dave named me Magellan, and after a few laughs we hiked on to Pedlar

Dam at Irish Creek, on the edge of a 5-acre preserve of 300-year-old Canadian hemlocks and virgin white pines. A blazing campfire and hot pasta made Lisa and me think we'd arrived at the Irish Creek Hilton after the previous night's ordeal.

The songbirds at dawn were Aaron Copland's "Appalachian Spring" come alive, reminding us that such a forest symphony will be minus its flute section if we don't preserve old-growth stands for future generations. The Forest Service has designated two wilderness areas in the Pedlar District, which stretches from the James River to Rockfish Gap. The Priest and Three Ridges areas are shielded from human encroachment, and Three Sisters will be maintained as a roadless area.

Sitting atop 3,862-foot-high Spy Rock in Virginia, Martha Ezzard (left) and her son, John Ezzard Jr., take a lunch break. He wears a leg brace because of recent knee surgery. Photo by David Tulis, Atlanta Journal-Constitution

The next day, we had an easy hike to the Brown Mountain Creek shelter, where freed slaves formed an agricultural community in the late 1800s. As we crossed U.S. 60, we ran into Taft Hughes, the son of one of the legendary residents of the Brown Mountain community. "My mother was born a slave, just one month too soon," he told us. He still farms nearby, but when I asked how many acres he had, he laughed. "None," he replied. "Can't you see this land belongs to the Lord?"

Our third day's challenge, Bald Knob, was Lisa's favorite mountain. Unlike its neighbor, Cold Mountain, it's anything but bald. Along its steep ascent, white fringed phacelia, giant ferns and trailing arbutus waved at us in a soft wind as if we were their parade. Wishing for both daughters in the romance of that setting, I vowed to ask my daughter Shelly, the artist in our family, just how many shades of green there can be, anyway.

By the time my free-spirited daughter and I reached the end of our trek near Montebello, Virginia, we had covered a lot of talking territory. I wondered what made conversations about our frequently clashing views on careers, finances, relationships and other hot-button topics so much more harmonious on this outing. I decided it was because I wasn't lecturing her about her life; we were sharing our thoughts and respecting each other's differences.

After a night at the Sugartree Inn in Steele's Tavern—with real sheets, a shower and a stuffed quail dinner—I traded daughter for son and began an equally fascinating, but different, journey.

John Ezzard, 25, has a degree in history. He analyzes big-picture things rather than the small mysteries of nature that Lisa so cherishes.

A romantic at heart and a realist when necessary, John has a more detached perspective

Taft Hughes (left), 84, lives in Long Mountain Valley near Brown Mountain Creek, a community founded by freed slaves. Carolyn Skipper helps look after his farm. Photo by David Tulis, Atlanta Journal-Constitution

A hiker's best friend: After work, Aubrey Taylor often drives to the trail's intersection with U.S. 60 near Long Mountain to dispense sodas and beer. Photo by David Tulis, Atlanta Journal-Constitution

that enables him to seek economic and environmental balance in man's relationship to the land. We had lively discussions on the subject as the trail narrowed at the end of our journey, and housetops and common kudzu replaced wild beauty.

But 20th-century incursions seemed far away after we scaled Spy Rock, an historic

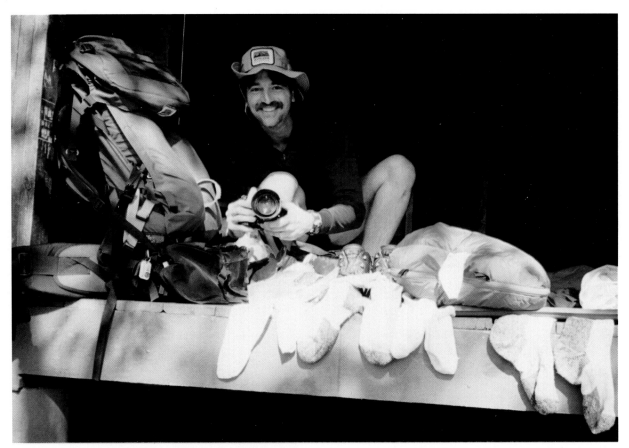

A plastic bag and biodegradable peppermint soap substitute for a washing machine as David Tulis seeks fresh socks at the Seeley-Woodworth shelter. Photo by David Tulis, Atlanta Journal-Constitution

Confederate lookout with a 360-degree view of mountains and forest. From there, John and I could glimpse a little of the privately owned Campbell property, surrounded by public land. Campbells settled in the 1700s and have farmed the land ever since. The three who dwell there now, all in their 60s, live isolated from the modern world, with no electricity, transportation or formal schooling.

From Spy Rock, we viewed the toughest challenges of our journey to come: the Priest and Three Ridges mountains. John and I were a great team on the 4,063-foot Priest. Age matters on steep ascents, and he cheered me on. A black-and-white warbler, whose song mimics a squeaky wheel, was my telling companion on the way up. For John, still wearing a brace from knee surgery last year, downhill was worse. I'd worried about his recovery before we started our journey. I knew that I'd

never forgive myself if the hike set him back. Despite my worries, he seemed more confident by the day.

If Lisa was my nurturer, John was my coach. After I'd scaled the last of the peaks of Three Ridges, 3,970 feet high and slick with rain, my son decided I deserved the title "he-mama."

From then on, we hiked, camped, ate, moved and breathed in wet everything. By the time we reached the jagged rocks of Humpback Mountain, I told John I'd had about all of the character-building I could stand.

But my weariness was secondary when John dumped his brace, which had rubbed his knee raw. Even as I slid over rock slides in some places and crawled on all fours over one, I worried more about him than about myself.

My son and I ended our soggy hike in a

field at the Blue Ridge Parkway at Rockfish Gap, longing simply for dry socks. Toasting our teamwork over a steak dinner that night, we looked back at a perfect rainbow over the mountains. And in the shared silence of that moment, I knew I'd been hiking with one of my life's most comfortable companions.

A DAUGHTER'S TALE

By Lisa Ezzard

Clichés sometimes work: "Women don't read maps—they just ask for directions." If we'd seen a fellow hiker we'd have asked, but we were too busy getting started, forging our own trail, chatting, catching up, as a mother and daughter do.

Unlike my father, who carries in his blood the knowledge of maps—the measurements of life, the meters, the scales, the charts, the tools—we were just "going" as our instincts would have it. And perhaps nature had something else in store for us when we missed a turn at the beginning of our trek.

We became lost in time, sucked into nature—following a wild turkey, listening for birdsong, skirting fallen trees. We chatted like birds ourselves, busy not with tools but with the relational meshings of our inner and outer worlds. Because the trail we were on was not a trail at all but an old logging road, we were able to walk next to each other and talk. We talked about children and families and religion. We defined "romantic."

Mom always says the South is romantic, as nature is. Sensual, actually. Suggestive . . . the long gloves, the hats, the smell of honeysuckle. My generation has never known romantic innocence, and I envy it.

I also envy Virginia's bouquets of flowers and its greenery. I grew up in Colorado, cre-

ating my own landscape of vast spaces, sparseness, rocks and big sky. I was unfamiliar with such gentleness of landscape, except in the way I had always been shown it through my mother. How lovely to see her personhood reflected in the hills and trees.

Who cares that we hiked 5 miles off track, lost our photographer, walked until nightfall and wound up with only a couple of mouthfuls of water to quench our thirst? In our "unawareness" we were returning to nature, and it was romantic.

APPALACHIAN HEAVEN

By Martha Ezzard

Tunnel of green, tunnel of green,
Soothe our souls with a thousand hues,
Black green of hemlock, chartreuse of fern,
Playing in patterns of sunlight and dusk.

Tunnel of green, tunnel of green,
Weave together life's disparate strands,
With arch of arbutus, song of thrush,
Cheering softly our fragile parade.

Tunnel of green, tunnel of green,
Temper steep challenge with spring's allure,
Touch jagged rock with dances of rain,
Wrap us in ribbons of see-through mist.

Tunnel of green, tunnel of green,
Drench our souls in running starlight,
White blazes summon from the sky,
To Katahdin, eternal Katahdin.

Colors reflected on Clark Creek.
Photo by Bill Wade, Pittsburgh
Post-Gazette

IT'S ALL DOWNHILL FROM HERE

M A Y 2 7 - J U L Y   8,   1 9 9 5

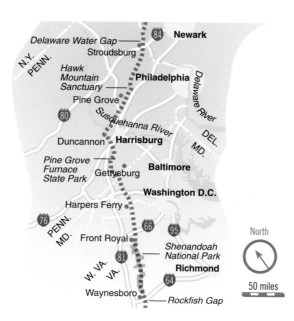

FRONT ROYAL, VIRGINIA

**Text by
Don Hopey**

**Photography by
Robin Rombach**

Afoot and lighthearted, I had stepped onto the Appalachian Trail 107 miles ago at the southern end of Shenandoah National Park. With a 45-pound pack on my back and Walt Whitman in my head, I was prepared to follow the long brown path "lose'd of limits and imaginary lines."

But the trail crosses Skyline Drive—the scenic roadway that displaced it along the Blue Ridge in 1939—27 times and swings close by at numerous other places. Those intersections make the trail easily accessible to the park's 2 million annual visitors but produce a truncated wilderness experience for the through-hiker.

At the northern end of the park near the Gravel Springs Hut, I rounded a bend to find a couple from Washington, D.C., in a tight embrace. She was in bedroom slippers, not hiking boots. Neither had any idea they were on the Appalachian Trail.

Jonny Lane (Squirrel Fight) of New Hampshire emerges from the woods to cross Skyline Drive in Shenandoah National Park.
Photo by Robin Rombach, Pittsburgh Post-Gazette

William E. Kendall (Mr. Ed) of Houston, Texas, follows the Appalachian Trail under a dead oak tree. A significant number of trees in the park are dying from infestation by insects such as the gypsy moth. Photo by Robin Rombach, Pittsburgh Post-Gazette

Andy Petras of Baltimore, who patrols the trail as a ridge runner for the Potomac Appalachian Trail Club, wasn't surprised by that story and recalled a surreal scene from his 1991 through-hike. He was eating lunch at one of the park's scenic overlooks off Skyline Drive when a Volvo containing two couples pulled in behind him.

"One of the two women in the car, in her best Barbara Walters voice, yelled into the back seat, 'Get out the video.' She then panned the woods, announcing into the microphone, 'This is the Appalachian Trail.' Then she turned the camera on me and said, 'This is an Appalachian Trail through-hiker.'

I just looked at her and said, 'Sorry, no interviews today,' grabbed up my lunch and pack and headed off up the trail."

Sandy Rives, south district leader in Shenandoah National Park, said that's about as painful as the interactions between motorists and the self-propelled trekkers get. In his seven years at the park, he said, no hiker has been hit by a car, despite some close calls.

Rives said the park is used by through-hikers, day hikers and those who just drive around after paying a $5 entrance fee. "About 40 percent of our visitors never get out of their cars," he said.

They don't know what they're missing. In

the park, hikers' eyes are much better fed than those of the auto-tourists, who are confined to the black macadam ribbon of Skyline Drive and its scenic turnouts.

On clear days, that wheeled bunch can overlook the Virginia Piedmont, the Shenandoah Valley and as many ridges as will fit under the horizon. Appalachian Trail hikers have those breathtaking vistas plus the added details gleaned from walking through them.

With a trail blaze in sight on a stout oak ahead, I step past bird's-foot violets and the pink and white blossoms of mountain laurel in bloom. A few steps, and I am chest-high in white-flowered blackberry vines. In a month or so, hikers through this section will snack on the berries that will supplant the flowers, if the bears don't beat them to it. Around a granite outcrop and through a zillion-piece rock jigsaw puzzle that no one will ever put together, I search for a size-10 plot of flat ground on which to place the next footfall. Each rock protruding from the trail is a potential land mine for ankles and knees.

When trailside vegetation is sparse and the footing good, I steal glances left and right,

Trail markings

A double paint blaze—one above the other—is placed before turns, junctions and other areas that require hikers to be alert.

The trail is marked with 2-inch by 6-inch vertical white paint blazes. Blue blazes mark side trails. Usually these lead to shelters, water supplies or special view points.

The historic insignia of the Trail is a 4-inch, diamond-shaped, galvanized steel marker, bearing the Appalachian Trail monogram and legend. In 1931, galvanized sheet iron replaced the more expensive steel marker. The green-and-white three-sided marker of the National Scenic Trail System identifies the trail at road crossings and other access points.

STACY INNERST/Pittsburgh Post-Gazette

Secretary of the Interior Bruce Babbitt takes in the view at the Ivy Creek overlook in Shenandoah National Park. Photo by Robin Rombach, Pittsburgh Post-Gazette

scanning the woods for one of the park's 600 Yogis. I haven't seen a bear but keep hearing from hikers who have. Deer are much more common; each day I spot a dozen or so along the trail or circling the huts at dusk and dawn. The bucks are in velvet, their antlers just coming in. Another step and there are wild azaleas, columbines, and Dutchman's-breeches, all in bloom. To the left two rufous-sided towhees cavort. Identified by their black, or if female, brown topside, white belly and rufous (Latin for red) flank, towhees often hop from bush to bush just ahead of hikers.

I put my hiking stick over a downed tree and follow, brushing aside some Virginia creeper that looks very similar to poison ivy

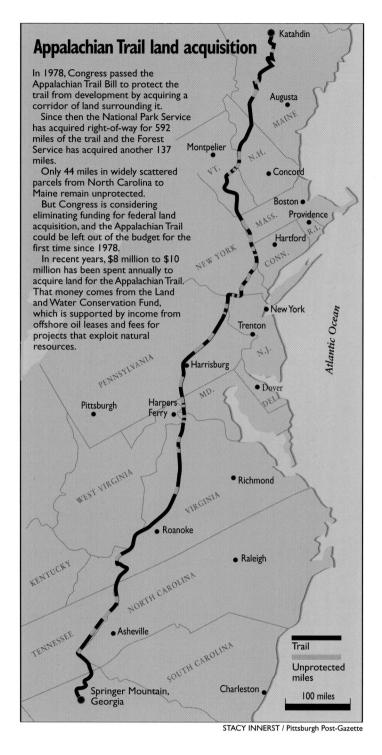

Appalachian Trail land acquisition

In 1978, Congress passed the Appalachian Trail Bill to protect the trail from development by acquiring a corridor of land surrounding it.

Since then the National Park Service has acquired right-of-way for 592 miles of the trail and the Forest Service has acquired another 137 miles.

Only 44 miles in widely scattered parcels from North Carolina to Maine remain unprotected.

But Congress is considering eliminating funding for federal land acquisition, and the Appalachian Trail could be left out of the budget for the first time since 1978.

In recent years, $8 million to $10 million has been spent annually to acquire land for the Appalachian Trail. That money comes from the Land and Water Conservation Fund, which is supported by income from offshore oil leases and fees for projects that exploit natural resources.

Trail
Unprotected miles
100 miles

STACY INNERST / Pittsburgh Post-Gazette

except for its five-leaf clusters. I use my stick again to push aside some tall grass and stinging nettles, now grown thigh-high in places. Undergrowth problems along the trail are becoming increasingly common because of numerous breaks in the tree canopy, which allow sunlight to reach the forest floor.

Those canopy breaks come from dead and dying trees; insects are killing the oaks, white pines and hemlocks. In places, the dead trees are so numerous that hillsides appear gray in midsummer. Park officials warn hikers not to camp under the dead trees and to be careful if they're out during storms. A limb from a dead tree fell and badly injured a park employee last year.

Another step and I am abreast of the blaze, then past it. The next is up ahead on a yellow poplar. Before I get there my consideration of a spray of trailside bluets and a scarlet tanager winging through a stand of live oaks is disrupted by the hum of steel-belted tires on macadam.

David Heinstadt (Red Fox), a through-hiker from Baltimore, said the park was not the wilderness experience he expected. "One thing I've learned is you can't fight the trail," he said during a hiking break as he tamped his pipe tobacco. "It can give you solitude or not."

In the Shenandoahs, the interaction between wilderness and people was planned. Established in 1926 in a heavily settled and clear-cut area, the park was an early effort to preserve nature in the urbanized east. Now 95 percent of the park is forested and almost half of its 195,000 acres have been designated wilderness.

Three days into our hike, Robin and I came upon the Secretary of the Interior in his natural habitat—a national park.

Bruce Babbitt, former Arizona governor and the Clinton administration's granola guy on environmental issues, was in the park to hike with us for a day and play a little defense against congressional proposals that he said threatened the future of the nation's park system.

"There's a debate going on about the future of the public park system, about terminating public space and selling it off for

(Left to right) Michel Pelletier (Fur Trapper), Tanner Critz (Wayah) and Squirrel Fight stop for a view at Loft Mountain in the Shenandoah National Park. The three are part of a larger group of young hikers who called themselves the "young Vikings." Photo by Robin Rombach, Pittsburgh Post-Gazette

whatever people want to do with it, be it mining or timbering or whatever, and the Appalachian Trail is a part of that," Babbitt said after meeting us at Browns Gap. Excavations here in 1985 found evidence that ancient Native American chiefs and medicine men performed ceremonies to ensure a bountiful hunt.

Proposed cuts to the Interior Department's budget and a five-year moratorium on land acquisition could result in the loss of sections of the 2,158-mile-long trail, Babbitt said. Since 1978, federal funding for land acquisition along the trail has averaged $8 million annually, and the 800 miles of trail located on

private land in 1978 have since been reduced to less than 44 miles spread over 14 states.

Several individuals in Maryland and the Killington and Pico Peak ski resorts in Vermont have balked at park service attempts to reroute or purchase land for the trail. In spite of these efforts, land acquisition for the corridor has stirred little controversy. Only 5 percent of all acquisitions have resulted from condemnation proceedings.

"Cuts to the Appalachian Trail land-acquisition program are part of a broader movement in Congress to roll back environmental successes. Who ever thought it would come to the national park system? But it has," Bab-

Rappellers climb down the rocks of Little Stony Man Mountain Overlook in Shenandoah National Park. Photo by Robin Rombach, Pittsburgh Post-Gazette

bitt said near the end of our day's hike in Pinefield Gap. "They view this park as just another attack point."

Shenandoah National Park and other preserves in the national park system offer unique outdoor opportunities for many people. "A scenic drive is a beginning, but only a first step," Babbitt said. "The real job is to lure people out of their cars and into direct contact, where they can see the sights and hear the birds and listen to the running water and begin to identify plants and animals."

During our day on the trail we passed a family with four young boys on a nature walk. Then we met a pair of through-hikers, Jonny Lane (Squirrel Fight) of Manchester, New Hampshire, and Michel Pelletier (Fur Trapper) of Chicago, who after three months out are, Babbitt observed, "blending into the woods like white-tailed deer.

"There's room for everybody," he said. "There's a challenging experience for everybody, from a three-year-old kid to a technical rock climber and that is absolutely the way it ought to be. That's the ultimate success of the national park system."

After 800 miles or so, most through-hikers are more than willing to share the trail and even enjoy an occasional taste of civilization. They're tired of freeze-dried Mandarin-orange chicken dinners, "mac 'n' cheese," and Little Debbie granola bars.

Shenandoah National Park allows hikers to break that monotony.

They lust after the cheeseburgers at the park's Loft Mountain Wayside and Grill, Klondike ice-cream bars from the cooler in the Big Meadows store, the Virginia ham-and-egg breakfasts at the Skyland Lodge restaurant, fried chicken and beer at the restaurant in Panorama and blackberry milk shakes from the Elkwallow Wayside and Grill. If their budgets can handle it—and sometimes even if they can't—many

Hikers John Zavodny (Turn Signal) (left) and Robert Mack (Lightning Hopkins) (middle) from Knoxville, Tennessee, and Don Hopey take a break from hiking through Shenandoah National Park. Photo by Robin Rombach, Pittsburgh Post-Gazette

through-hikers plan their hikes and meals around the temptations.

At the Rock Springs Hut, a register entry by Chris Hart (Dances with Snakes) of Milford, Massachusetts, states flatly: "This park is doing a good job of spoiling me. The food bag hasn't lost any weight."

Later, outside the Elkwallow Wayside, Dances with Snakes is more expansive with a beer in his hand. "This is luxury hiking, no

Sandy Grice of Norfolk, Virginia, who is a volunteer with the Potomac Appalachian Trail Club, paints a white blaze on a rock on Bear Den Mountain. Photo by Robin Rombach, Pittsburgh Post-Gazette

▲ **T r a i l   M i x —**
We were picking and eating ripe wild strawberries on the bald of Bear Den Mountain when we came upon a man painting a bright white blaze on a stone cairn. It was like catching Santa Claus filling a Christmas stocking.

As we approached, and Robin Rombach began snapping photos, Sandy Grice turned and smiled a cherubic smile. "Hey," he shouted, "don't take a picture of this one. It's not my best." Grice, a real-estate appraiser from Norfolk, Virginia, has been taking care of the 3-mile section of trail between McCormick Gap and Beagle Gap for 17 years. He repaints the blazes once every seven or eight years. ▲

doubt," he said, "and it's real nice to get a taste of civilization after hiking about halfway, to relax and enjoy the national-park tourist thing, but I'm glad it's over. I'm looking forward to getting back to the real woods."

John Zavodny (The Hiker Formerly Known as John or Turn Signal), a graduate student in philosophy at the University of Tennessee in Knoxville, said his park hike was no wilderness experience. "I'm used to hiking in the Smokies, where you can spend 10 days hiking and cross one road, and that doesn't have a grocery store," said Zavodny. "It's nice to take advantage of these waysides, but part of what I like about being in the woods is giving up control. Here you know if you walk up or off a ridge, 50 yards later you'll be on Skyline Drive."

Still, there are pockets in the park where all you can hear are whippoorwills and rufous-sided towhees, all you can see ahead are trail markings, all you feel is freedom and good fortune. Whitman had it right.

On Little Stony Man Mountain we hiked past an outing club whose members were rappelling from the

Through-hiker Bill Cleveland (Doc Vapor) of Atlanta, Georgia, soaks his sore feet in the cool water of Ivy Creek. Photo by Robin Rombach, Pittsburgh Post-Gazette

Radio-transmission towers loom in the fog at the top of Bear Den Mountain, just outside of Rockfish Gap, Virginia, as Don Hopey climbs.
Photo by Robin Rombach, Pittsburgh Post-Gazette

granite cliffs. Bill Cleveland (Doc Vapor) of Atlanta observes that rock climbing is "a much more attractive sport than backpacking, except for the cliffs and rocks." ▲

It falls to me to write the final, bittersweet chapter in the Appalachian Trail saga of Pearl Drops and Keebler. In a bit of serendipity, we walked into the HoJo's at Rock Fish Gap to fill our water bottles just as Pearl Drops and Keebler were walking off the trail for the final time. The beginning of the end occurred a month ago when the pair took time off for a visit to their home in

Franklin County, Virginia. They returned to the trail, but their hearts didn't. "We're getting off because Keebler is homesick," Pearl Drops told us during a tearful meeting that was both hello and good-bye. "Also, I'm getting married. I got engaged when I went home. The wedding is set for November 4."

Keebler looked 10 pounds lighter but a whole head taller than when last we'd met. He'd also grown in other ways. Asked what he'd learned during his three-month walk in the woods, he said, "It's important not to go so fast that you miss the flowers. I always have to remind my mom." ▲

HARPERS FERRY, WEST VIRGINIA

If this Civil War shrine is Oz for wayfarers on the Appalachian Trail, and it is, then Jean Cashin must be Glinda.

After walking for nearly 1,000 miles, hikers are ready to kick back. Many grab a couple of days off to recharge and resupply when

Since 1979, it has been tradition for through-hikers to have Jean Cashin take Polaroid pictures of them in front of the Appalachian Trail Conference building. Tony Dus (foreground) and Rich Sprow joke with Cashin after their picture session. Photo by Robin Rombach, Pittsburgh Post-Gazette

they reach this town that seems to defy gravity by clinging to the steep hillsides where the Shenandoah and Potomac Rivers rush to meet.

Here they also meet Cashin. Like the good witch of Oz, she has fashioned a 23-year career at the Appalachian Trail Conference out of pointing storm-tossed and confused travelers in the right direction.

For many hikers, Cashin's is the first voice of encouragement they hear when they begin planning their hikes. A visit to Appalachian Trail Conference headquarters, in the tiny

town where John Brown led a short-lived slave revolt that helped to trigger the Civil War, is an opportunity for them to put a face with the name.

"Say 'sex,'" the 65-year-old grandmother says from under a shock of thick gray hair as she snaps a Polaroid of several through-hikers outside conference headquarters.

Since 1979, it has been a holy ritual for through-hikers to have Cashin take their pictures in front of the two-story white-stucco building. Back inside, she asks them how their hike is going. They respond with a thumbs-up. She returns the gesture and adds a smile. "That's the glory of being here for so long," Cashin said. "The reward of the job is talking to people who are so happy. I actually see them healed mentally and physically. I don't know anyone that's set out to do the trail that hasn't been affected, and I don't know that I'm ever going to be able to leave." Not that anyone's asking her to. Her memory and sense of humor are legendary, a tough-to-beat combination when your job title is information specialist and your desk sits right inside the front door.

"She's the Earth Mother of the trail," said Karen Lutz, the conference's mid-Atlantic regional representative. "She can make it seem like your question is the first she's ever had about a certain trail subject even though she's heard and answered it 6,000 times before."

Lutz, who through-hiked in 1978, remembers walking into the Harpers Ferry

Kenneth Mick (Two Feet) of Tallahassee, Florida, hikes through a field of an old farm near the Denton shelter outside Fort Royal, Virginia.
Photo by Robin Rombach, Pittsburgh Post-Gazette

headquarters and announcing that she was taking a break and needed a ride to the train station in Frederick, Maryland. Cashin drove her.

"She's the front line for people contacts at the conference office," she said. "When you call and ask 'Where can I get water on the trail in Connecticut?' she'll know or put you in contact with someone who does."

The hectic days outnumber the slow ones now, as membership in the conference has grown from 6,000 in 1972 to nearly 26,000 today, and more and more people are finding their way to the white blazes. The conference coordinates trail maintenance, provides information and publishes maps and guides.

As good as she is at juggling phones, Cashin seems to relish the walk-in traffic more, even when she can smell it a block or two away. "Friday we had a lot of through-hikers come in, and it smelled like a zoo in here," she said. The can of Lysol she keeps under her desk got heavy use.

Aside from the increase in the number of hikers, Cashin said the biggest change she's noticed is in the commitment of those who pass through the conference headquarter's doors.

Don Hopey (left) and Lightning Hopkins look for dens of rattlesnakes at Buzzard's Rocks, high above the town of Shannondale in West Virginia. Photo by Robin Rombach, Pittsburgh Post-Gazette

A black snake makes an appearance along the trail near Harpers Ferry, West Virginia. Photo by Robin Rombach, Pittsburgh Post-Gazette

"I don't know if you call them idealists today, but there are so many young people who care about the environment and about this fantastic resource. Most of them have done a major part of the trail or all of it, and they get out every summer and work with the trail crews. The hike probably changed their lives and it's pay-back time."

Although Cashin has been an avid day hiker, she hasn't through-hiked the trail. "I'm not crazy," she said with a laugh.

After giving hiking advice for 23 years, Cashin can boil her wisdom down to two words: "Be prepared." Plan the hike. Get good guidebooks and maps. Talk to someone who's done it. Test your equipment before you go. Wear good boots.

"It's not a cup of tea out there," she said. "It's often painful. It hurts. You know that already, and you ain't seen nothing yet. Wait until you get to the rocks in Pennsylvania."

Cashin was right. The trail leading into Harpers Ferry was no yellow-brick road. On one 18-mile day from Sky Meadows State Park to the hostel on Bears Den Mountain, the trail seesawed in and out of a succession of hollows and ridges, forcing Robin and

me to climb close to 5,000 vertical feet.

And spring has run out on us. Summer has caught up. In the valleys a honeysuckle fog plays in our noses, but on the higher ridges only the white flowers of the mountain laurel and pink primrose break up the deep green of the woods. Stinging nettles, poison ivy and briars crowd along many sections of the trail in northern Virginia.

One of the highlights of the week's hike, during which we covered 53 miles, was the Potomac Appalachian Trail Club's Jim and Molly Denton shelter, just outside of Front Royal, Virginia. The Denton shelter is dubbed the "Hikers Hilton," and judging by hiker's comments in the shelter register, it's the best north-bounders have seen on the trail. Named for the Dentons, who met in 1942 as members of the Roanoke Appalachi-an Trail Club, the shelter has a separate cooking pavilion, barbecue pit, spring-fed shower *(Brrr!)*, deck and Adirondak-style bench chairs. Robin and I sat one evening and watched the first lightning bugs of the summer while we savored tea and a four-pack of Godiva truffles, the gift of a goddess, my wife Carole.

Hikers leave the woods to cross Interstate 70 in Maryland, near Washington, D.C. Photo by Robin Rombach, Pittsburgh Post-Gazette

We also spent a night at the Bears Den hostel at the summit of Bears Den Mountain. It is run by Bill Miller and Kelly Shea, who met while through-hiking last year. The Norman-style castle of locally quarried quartzite was built by a Washington, D.C., doctor for his opera-singer wife in 1933. The castle has since been transformed into a 20-bed hostel that offers a hot shower, a bunk, a sheet sleepsack, laundry facilities and cooking privileges in a well-equipped kitchen for $12 a night to conference members.

Our biggest adventure of the week came on a side trail to Buzzard Rocks, high above the town of Shannondale and the Shenandoah River in West Virginia. We had heard about dens of rattlesnakes there from an Englishman named Ed Mason (The Duke of Gorp). "Some as thick as a man's arm," he said. We had to go.

Led by Robert Mack (Lightning Hopkins) of Knoxville, Tennessee, our hiking companion for the last part of the week, we ventured onto the jumble of rocks. True to his name, Lightning Hopkins was 20 yards out into the granite and quartzite before he turned to report that there were no snakes.

Then I said, "Here's some," pointing to a crevice about 10 feet ahead of me that Hopkins had skipped over. Robin later said she

Don Hopey (left) helps hang glider Eric Wakefield take off for a flight from High Rock in Maryland, near the Pennsylvania border and the Mason-Dixon line. Photo by Robin Rombach, Pittsburgh Post-Gazette

could tell by my voice that I wasn't kidding. Lightning Hopkins said "No way!" and hoped I was.

Two or possibly three rattlers were in a tight pretzel knot between my boulder and the next one. When they began to writhe in all directions at once and a rattle and two heads appeared, we beat a hasty retreat. "What a rush, man," Lightning Hopkins said as we hiked on. "If we had this adrenaline to hike on all day, we'd be in Harpers Ferry this afternoon."

Or we could just click the heels of our hiking boots together.

Don Hopey crosses a log bridge over Falls Creek in Pennsylvania near the Mason-Dixon line. Photo by Robin Rombach, Pittsburgh Post-Gazette

Wildlife along the central trail

As hikers move north on the Appalachian Trail, they continue to see some of the same animals that inhabit the trail's southern end, such as the white-tailed deer and ruffed grouse, while encountering some new fauna, such as brook trout and the timber rattlesnake.

Brook trout
Found in cold, clear streams, such as James River in Virginia and Yellow Breeches Creek in Pennsylvania. Fishing along the trail is permitted with a state fishing license.

White-tailed deer
Deer are plentiful along the length of the trail because of the absence of their natural predators, wolves and mountain lions. During the spring and summer you're likely to see a newborn fawn with its mother, or a buck "in velvet" with its developing antlers covered with a fuzzy, protective skin.

NEW YORK

Timber rattlesnake
Most trail sightings of rattlers are in Viirginia and Pennsylvania. Dry, rocky areas are their favorite haunts, and most of their hunting is done at night. Their favorite food is mice, not humans, so bites are rare and seldom fatal.

NEW JERSEY

● Delaware Water Gap

Gray fox
If you see a fox on your trek, it will likely be a gray fox, which prefers wooded areas and can be found along the length of the A.T. About the size of a small dog, it's the only member of the dog family capable of climbing trees.

PENNSYLVANIA

● Pittsburgh

Harpers Ferry

VIRGINIA

Ruffed grouse
Can be found in mixed or deciduous forests along the central trail. Identified by a small crest and a fan-shaped tail edged with black and white. The male makes a distinctive drumming sound with his wings as part of the courtship display.

100 miles

N

Shenandoah National Park

WEST VIRGINIA

Black bear
Most commonly seen in the Shenandoah National Park, sightings usually result in the bear dashing into the bush. Their diet consists mainly of plant material but they will eat meat in the form of small animals such as snakes, frogs, salamanders and mice. They are also fond of hiker food.

STACY INNERST / Pittsburgh Post-Gazette

▲ T r a i l   M i x —
In addition to the rattlers, we were also able to check eastern box turtles, turkeys, newts, toads and sable antelope off our Animal Bingo cards. The antelope, some sporting only one horn so they resembled stocky, shaggy unicorns, are native to southern Africa but are among the many wild and weird species penned in the Smithsonian's National Zoological Park Conservation and Research Center along both sides of Route 522 outside Front Royal, Virginia. ▲

This was a very successful week for "yogi-ing"—a trail term for getting offers of food or assistance without asking for it. Just by looking particularly beat after an 18-mile day in 90-plus-degree temperatures, Robin and I were able to yogi half a roasted chicken from a Washington, D.C., couple at the Bears Den hostel and a big pot of vegetarian chili from Bill Miller and Kelly Shea. When we arrived in Harpers Ferry, we visited Al and Allison Alsdorf, owners of the Harpers Ferry Guest House Bed & Breakfast, across the street from the Appalachian Trail Conference headquarters. I yogied drinks, cookies and Allison's car for an afternoon of errand running. ▲

The view from the trail of a Potomac River gorge at Weaverton Cliffs is near Harpers Ferry, West Virginia. Photo by Robin Rombach, Pittsburgh Post-Gazette

Sarah Desjardins (Which Way), of South Dartmouth, Massachusetts and David Heinstadt (Red Fox), from Baltimore, Maryland at the half-way marker of the trail at Pine Grove Furnace State Park. Photo by Bill Wade, Pittsburgh Post-Gazette

MOUNT HOLLY SPRINGS, PENNSYLVANIA

It's all downhill from here.

That's a through-hiker's joke. No one who has reached the midpoint of this 2,158-mile hump along the spine of the Appalachians believes it for a millisecond.

For all of us north-bounders, Pennsylvania's infamous ridge-top rock fields loom ahead, and the White Mountains await in New England.

Still, there is a sense that the halfway sign on the Appalachian Trail, on an uphill hike out of Pine Grove Furnace State Park, is more than just another mile marker.

From mid-Maryland north, the evidence of this excitement can be found in shelter registers. The books we have seen have been awash with philosophical reflections on the trail and ice-cream lust in anticipation of Pine Grove Furnace Park store, traditional home of the "Half-Gallon Club."

Membership in this exclusive club is open to anyone who has hiked there from Georgia or Maine with $3.80 in their pocket for a half gallon of Hershey's ice cream and the voracity to eat the whole thing in one sitting. Tony Paliometros, the store owner, gives each new member a small wooden spoon to commemorate his or her ice-cream-induced head- and stomachaches.

"The halfway point means we start counting miles backwards," said through-hiker David Heinstadt (Red Fox), 34, from Baltimore, shortly after finishing off a half gallon of coffee ice cream. "Instead of saying how many miles we've come, we can start saying how many miles we have to go."

Robin and I covered 91 trail miles last week, traipsing from West Virginia through Maryland and into Pennsylvania. In Maryland, we hiked along the backbone of South Mountain to a breathtaking view of the Potomac River gorge from Weaverton Cliffs. We had a vertigo-inducing excursion out to

Black Rock Cliffs to see a 180-degree panorama—considered the trail's best in Maryland—where lightning from an approaching thunderstorm caused our hair to stand on end.

Throughout the week we passed mountains full of white mountain laurels slightly past their peak but still draping the woods like an unseasonal snowfall. More prevalent than the laurels was the feeling among hikers that they were turning a corner. "This is the first time I've done this many miles, and I'll be psyched when I walk up the trail and hit that sign," said Wayne Jones (Joker) of Lancaster County, Pennsylvania.

For some, making it halfway to Mount Katahdin in Maine is exhilarating; for others, daunting. It is a time for both celebration and reflection.

After treating themselves to a stay in the Highland House Bed and Breakfast, which overlooks Boiling Springs Lake in Pennsylvania, Red Fox and Doc Vapor are ready to move on. Photo by Bill Wade, Pittsburgh Post-Gazette

In the trail register at the halfway signpost, John Bevans (Jones) of Rochester, New York, wrote: "Congratulations to all in front and in back. This is a milestone we all should be proud to be a part of."

But while we were hiking together just a day earlier, Jones admitted that he had mixed feelings. "We're halfway, and I don't know if I feel half-empty or half-full. I'm happy it's half-done, but it's another step toward finishing and I don't want this to end.

"I'd like to stay out here a long time."

By getting out into the woods, away from phones, friends and family, hikers have given themselves an opportunity to reflect on some life decisions. Many besides Jones find themselves halfway through a journey of personal discovery with questions still unanswered.

There is still time. And space. Out here where hikers carry their houses on their backs, they can simplify things, strip away distractions, listen to inner voices, think without being interrupted. That's how Anthony Dus (Sir Renity) of Pittsfield, Massachusetts says he used the first 1,079 miles. "For me the trip is more mental housekeeping than mileage. The miles don't mean that much," he said. "Over the last month I've done a lot of thinking, and I've been able to get the living room and bedroom clean. Now I'm working on the bathroom. That's the worst."

As I reached the midpoint signpost, my biggest discovery was a reaffirmation of a sometimes forgotten belief in the basic goodness of people. Time and time again, starting even before I set foot on the trail at Rock Fish Gap, Virginia, I have witnessed and experienced acts of kindness that hikers refer to as "trail magic," but which on a basic level are just human-size encounters in which people watch out for one another.

The latest in a long line of examples came last Friday when I awoke at Penn-Mar County Park on the Pennsylvania-Maryland border with a little toe that Robin said looked like a boiled Vienna sausage. It had been hurting for three days and wasn't getting any better. We decided to hike 3 miles to the next road crossing and hitch to the hospital emergency room in Waynesboro, Maryland, 5 miles away.

Val Korszniak (Korsz) of Mount Laurel, New Jersey, reads a newspaper in front of the Doyle Hotel in Duncannon, Pennsylvania. A stay at the 100-year-old hotel, which charges $10 for a single, is a hiker tradition. Photo by Bill Wade, Pittsburgh Post-Gazette

Trail priorities being what they are—food first, then feet—we stopped at a diner in Blue Ridge Summit for breakfast. In a bit of kismet, we discovered a medical clinic across the street that was open only on Friday mornings. I limped over. Dr. Diana J. Lyon-Loftus examined my infected toe. She drained it, dressed it, told me to stay off it and wrote a prescription for antibiotics.

One problem was that the pharmacy in Blue Ridge Summit couldn't fill the prescription and I would have to go to Waynesboro. The other problem was that we were scheduled to hike 15 miles to Caledonia State Park.

The good doctor not only drove us to the pharmacy but also picked us up after I got the prescription filled and fed us fresh fruit, yogurt and juice as she drove us to Caledonia State Park, where she recommended that I soak the foot for the day in the park's swimming pool.

Some days on the Appalachian Trail, it seems the miles are all downhill.

▲ Trail Mix—
After carrying a fly rod through Shenandoah National Park and three states without so much as making a cast, I was finally able to float a mayfly imitation over some hungry brook trout on the East Branch of Conococheague Creek in Caledonia State Park. ▲

The wildest sanctioned event on the trail has to be the one-day hike covering four states and 42 miles, staged every two years in May by the Mountain Club of Maryland. Hikers start at first light in northern Virginia and move rapidly through West Virginia and Maryland's 38-mile neck before crossing the Mason-Dixon line into Pennsylvania.

Thurston Griggs, who patrols the Maryland section, said 83 hikers participated in the last four-state hike and all but seven made it. "I've done it once myself, but that was a few years ago when I was younger," said the 80-year-old ridge runner. ▲

PINE GROVE, PENNSYLVANIA

Photography by Bill Wade

We were supposed to hike lily-bedecked valleys and rocky ridgetops with Earl Shaffer, but he never showed.

A resident of York Springs, just a few miles from where we started hiking this week, Shaffer is to the Appalachian Trail what Babe Ruth was to baseball: a man who changed the game.

He was the first person to through-hike the trail, Georgia to Maine, in 1948. He became the first to hike it in both directions when he completed a 99-day Maine-to-Georgia stroll in 1965. To one degree or another, everyone out here is following in his footsteps. It would have been a

trip to walk with him along some of the 82 trail miles that my new trail companion, photographer Bill Wade, and I traveled this week in Pennsylvania and to hear his thoughts about today's long-ball hikers and how the trail has changed.

But Shaffer's 76-year-old hip was acting up on him, or maybe it was his Volkswagen minibus, or his memory. "That's just the way Earl is," said his friend George Anderson, who lives near Boiling Springs and offered the smorgasbord of excuses. "He's a recluse."

Whatever. When you're a recluse, appointments really don't fit the definition.

It would have been nice to have heard Shaffer's thoughts on all the trail relocations in the Cumberland Valley, north of picturesque Boiling Springs, the one-time iron-mining village locals call Bubbletown.

When Shaffer did his through-hikes, the trail ran mostly along roads. Now, after land purchases or hard-fought battles to win ease-

Clay Crowder (Clay) of Marietta, Georgia, warms himself with a hot beverage in the Darlington shelter after hiking all day in the rain. Photo by Bill Wade, Pittsburgh Post-Gazette

North of Duncannon, Pennsylvania, Don Hopey walks with his bamboo hiking stick along the section of the trail that hikers call Rocksyl-vania. Photo by Bill Wade, Pittsburgh Post-Gazette

ments, Bill and I followed a different, more pastoral route through fields of wheat, corn and clover. In thickets between the farm fields, purple thistles and orange day lilies fought with pungent honeysuckle vines for space, and I picked early ripe raspberries from the sunniest spots.

Bruce Dunlavy, another hiker friend of Shaffer's and a "trail angel" who helps hikers find beds, breakfasts and beers around Boiling Springs and Carlisle, told me, "You should count yourself lucky to have talked to him once."

We met Shaffer earlier this spring at his tiny homestead, next to a verdant meadow his goats keep neatly trimmed, and behind the barn in which he refurbishes antiques and cannibalizes three VW buses to keep a fourth running, sometimes. His home, just a two-

room shed, has no running water, electricity or phone.

Shaffer appeared out of the woods beyond the meadow. Alhough in his mid-70s, he looked 20 years younger—until he smiled, revealing a row of dental neglect. He told me he weighs just what he did in high school and hasn't had to visit a doctor in 50 years. His health secret is a daily tablespoon of vinegar. And he had "the bright eyes"—that twinkly, distant horizon focus often found on the faces of through-hikers. His trail name was Crazy One. He joked that the second man to through-hike the trail was "Crazy Too." Though his once-thick black thatch has thinned, he still talks of through-hiking the trail one more time.

He has used his simple lifestyle and chosen solitude to become well read, and is well spoken on a variety of subjects from gardening to politics to beekeeping to religion. Friends say he plays a mean guitar. He is a composer, a poet and an author. His journal of the first through-hike, *Walking with Spring*, is a trail classic.

His love for the trail is legendary, although, he believes, unrequited. "I'd have been better off if I'd never done the trail. I'd have had more to show for my life," Shaffer said, briefly displaying the psychological bruises from his battles with the Appalachian Trail Conference. He believes the conference double-crossed him by letting him work for six years to establish a hostel on the trail near

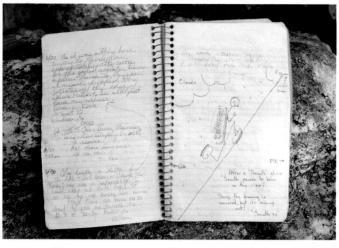

Hikers use the journals at trail shelters, trail heads and other major stops to communicate with one another, but many hikers also keep personal records of their thoughts and drawings. Pictured here is a typical entry by Keith Dailey (Smooth) of Glengary, West Virginia, (right page) and Clay Crowder (left page). Photo by Bill Wade, Pittsburgh Post-Gazette

Mount Holly Springs before canceling the project.

His friend Anderson said Shaffer, along with trail pioneers Milton Avery and Benton McKaye, lobbied hard in Washington during the 1950s to obtain protections for the trail. "But the conference was ultimately too political for him," Anderson said. "That's why he got burned."

In the years after his hikes, Shaffer helped relocate many segments of the trail. He also built or helped to build a half-dozen shelters, including the Thelma Marks Memorial shelter on Cove Mountain where two hikers were killed by a transient three years ago. We stopped by the shelters to get water from the nearby spring and to pay our respects. Judging by the shelter register entries, many hikers did the same. Few stayed the night.

In Duncannon, once "the jewel of the Susquehanna," we stayed at the Doyle Hotel, built around 1900 by the Anheuser-Busch Company and legendary in hiking circles for its 50-cent draft beers. Most of the pioneer hikers stayed there, although we were unable to locate Shaffer's name in any of the early hiker registers at the bar.

Although peeling and frayed around the edges, the Doyle offers hikers a rare chance to mix with locals who are friendly even when they've been displaced from their regular bar stools. On the evening that we sampled a few Yuengling Black & Tans, a regular patron had a baby hawk perched on his shoulder and handed the bird around to hikers. "The Doyle, where the beers are almost free and the drunks are loyal," was the poetic summary of Mike Kamph of Canton, Ohio, whose trail name is Joker.

Out of Duncannon we climbed 750 vertical feet up Peters Mountain, overlooking the Susquehanna River, and I would have liked to have heard Shaffer's comments on the canted, ankle-turning, tabletop-size rock outcroppings on top. They certainly hadn't changed much in the almost 50 years since that first hike.

Early the next morning, also on Peters Mountain, I saw my first black bear of the hike, a burly bruin that ambled across the trail 20 yards in front of me before crashing

Don Hopey climbs—in 90° temperatures—the rocks leading to Center Point Knob, near Boiling Springs, Pennsylvania, also known as Bubbletown. Photo by Bill Wade, Pittsburgh Post-Gazette

A view of Pennsylvania farmland near New Tripoli Campsite in Schuylkill County. Photo by Bill Wade, Pittsburgh Post-Gazette

noisily through the sassafras and oak saplings and down off the ridge. Shaffer would have enjoyed that.

And had he been with me at the Peters Mountain shelter the evening before, he would have seen thousands of fireflies twinkling along the trail and deep, deep into a woods made more magical by their love lights. I'm sure Shaffer's bright eyes would have twinkled back.

▲ Trail Mix—

Among Earl's pearls on trail travel: "Be careful late. After a full day of hiking, when you're tired, that's when accidents happen."

The most important piece of equipment on the trail is your mental state. "Your mind is a computer, always calculating the next step. It's what keeps you from getting hurt and injured. It's what keeps you comfortable and happy."

When you're carrying a heavy pack, hiking at a 2 mph pace is harder than hiking at 3 mph. At the slower pace, you're lugging the weight of the pack with every step. At 3 mph, the faster hiking rhythm provides momentum that helps carry the pack along.

The perfect hiking hat is a pith helmet. "It's cool, it's a hard hat to protect you from tree branches and it sheds rain and shields you from the sun." ▲

LEHIGH GAP, PENNSYLVANIA

Rock and Roll. Rolling Rock. Rock Bass. Rock of Ages. Rock candy. Rocky Balboa.

After scrambling, slipping, scraping, stumbling, spraining and stubbing my way through jagged gray-green quartzite shards ranging in size from pork chops to pumpkins to Plymouths, I thought that if I named them, the rocks might be nicer to me. Rocky Raccoon. Rocket man. Rock Lobster. Crocodile Rock. Rock and Rye. Roxanne. Ouch! Damn rocks!

The rocks in the Keystone State have my full attention, and the attention of everyone who sets foot on the trail north from Duncannon. Hikers know the state as "Rocksylvania," and the stretch through the northeast as "90 miles of hell."

For most of the 66 miles Bill and I hiked this week, it felt as though I were walking in a stream bed full of live, hungry piranhas that were biting at my feet each step of the way. Between the Eckville hostel at the base of Hawk Mountain and the Bake Oven Knob shelter, south of Lehigh Gap, we hiked 19 miles in one day, and I do not remember taking a step in which I did not feel a rock of some size and sharpness underneath my boots.

As a result, my dogs are bloody and barkin' bigtime. And they have company. "I hate the rocks," said Patrick Morrissey (High Plains Drifter), a hiker from Virginia Beach, Virginia, whose arches are sore. "I've been dreading them since Georgia."

"Those rocks knocked me out," William E. Kendall (Mr. Ed) of Houston said at the Eagle's Nest shelter just south of Port Clinton. His knee, hip and calf were all hurting. "I made a promise to my feet not to get on them again for 14 hours."

The rocks cut down the daily mileage hikers can do—and want to do—because each step is painful. Twenty-year-old Randy Evarts (Tenderfoot) of Newport, Maine, gets around on the rocks better than most mountain goats do, but even he has limitations.

"I don't mind the big rocks, because I enjoy hopping, but I hate the small, sharp stones," he said. "I wish I had a nickel or even a penny for every time I stubbed my toe in a day; I'd be a rich man. They're not very friendly."

Squirrel Fight shares food with another hiker in front of the Port Clinton Post Office. Many hikers mail food and other items ahead of themselves. Photo by Bill Wade, Pittsburgh Post-Gazette

This rocky walk along the Blue Mountain Ridge can claim a hiker's soul or soles. Clay Crowder's (Clay) new pair of $250 boots are on their way back to the manufacturer after he ripped them up in a boulder field south of Port

Don Hopey's blue pack and bamboo walking stick sit outside the Port Clinton Hotel. Photo by Bill Wade, Pittsburgh Post-Gazette

Clinton. In a hiker register near the Hawk Mountain Sanctuary, a couple of hiking days north, Crowder joked, "I hope there are more rocks ahead to push me to the edge of sanity."

Not to worry. There are plenty, and they've been around for a while. The quartzite was created more than 400 million years ago from glacial deposits of sand and turned on edge maybe 150 million years later when Africa played a little continental bump and run with North America. Just 2 million years ago, a series of freeze-and-thaw cycles began cracking the folded quartzite into the big angular blocks, slabs and wedges hikers now hop along on the Blue Mountain ridge.

The big jumbles present hikers with a combination of maze and trapezoidal fun house steps as they try to follow the trail's white blazes, which are often painted on the rocks because there are no trees available. Complicating matters for hikers is the discovery that many of the rocks, even the big ones, are "movers and shakers."

The rocks talk, according to Woodrow Murphy, the self-proclaimed "biggest guy on the trail" when he weighed in at 350 pounds on Springer Mountain in Georgia. He's dropped 53 pounds since but has picked up a conspiracy theory worthy of Oliver Stone. "The rocks are in conversation, and the slippery ones team up to stop hikers," said the Perrerell, Massachusetts native, whose trail name is Beorn. "Then there are the vampire rocks. They want your blood. There are the 'hip' rocks, that just want a little skin. And some rocks can jump.

Woody Goodwin (Woody), Clay and Joker relax at the newly built Peters Mountain shelter, north of Duncannon. The new shelter is just a stone's throw from a small, old log shelter once named for Earl Shaffer, the first through-hiker in 1948. But Shaffer requested his name be removed after a wooden floor was added. Photo by Bill Wade, Pittsburgh Post-Gazette

Jesse Kushner (Jericho), 24, from Madison, Wisconsin, eats her pasta-plus-something dinner at the Eagle's Nest shelter, west of Port Clinton. Photo by Bill Wade, Pittsburgh Post-Gazette

They grab your boot just when you think you've got it clear."

Because of the treacherous footing, hikers often complain that they see Pennsylvania three feet at a time because they have to focus on their next footfall. Once, after hiking

TOP: *Stephen Yingling (Trail Junkie) of Chillicothe, Ohio, gets water from his hiking partner Amy Dewey (Echo) of Cincinnati, Ohio, on Pulpit Rock near The Pinnacle northeast of Port Clinton.* Photo by Bill Wade, Pittsburgh Post-Gazette

BOTTOM: *Bill Wade's boots dry in the window of the Fine Lodging Hotel. The main street of Slatington, Pennsylvania, is in the background.* Photo by Bill Wade, Pittsburgh Post-Gazette

hickory and oak canopy on a forest floor carpeted wall to wall with lush ferns.

The week's hike actually offered a host of marvelous sights to those who took the time to look up. We had fine views of rolling Pennsylvania farmland and blue-hazed ridges from Pulpit Rock and The Pinnacle, northeast of Port Clinton. A little farther north we caught views and saw hawks riding updrafts from Knife Edge—scary because of its narrow traverse across a steeply canted outcrop—and Bear Rocks, which offers a 360-degree panorama after just a 10-minute scramble off the trail and up boulders ranging in size from refrigerators to tractor trailers.

Our only town visit of the week was in Port Clinton, which bears the un-Chamber of Commerce-like appellation "Buzzard Capital of the Northeast."

We stopped for a pop at the Port Clinton Hotel, where Helen Carbaugh has held forth for 30 years. Helen limits hikers to two, or if she's feeling kindly, three, of her seven-ounce, 55-cent Yuengling drafts. "You're here to hike, not to become a drunk," she said, and passed around salt and slices of raw parsnip from her garden.

On our way out of Port Clinton, we skirted the side of Hawk Mountain. Once a popular hunting ground for bird hunters, the site was converted into the Hawk Mountain

without lifting my head for about 15 minutes near the Pocahontas Campsite north of Port Clinton, I stopped and looked around—the prudent sequence rather than the other way around. I found myself under a pretty maple,

Sanctuary in 1934 for the study of the more than 14 species of hawks, falcons and eagles that use the mountain's strong updrafts to carry them south for the winter. Peak viewing months are September and October.

Near the end of our hiking week, on the North Trail, a scenic side trail on the ridge above Palmerton, just south of Lehigh Gap, we had a clear view of the Lehigh River valley and the mountainsides denuded by the pollution of a century of zinc-mining and smelting operations. The area, now an Environmental Protection Agency Superfund cleanup site, is slowly being revegetated. Pines, tall grasses and blueberry bushes are taking hold.

It was a pleasure to look down and see, for at least a short while, handfuls of tasty ripe berries instead of rocks.

▲ Trail Mix—
After walking through four states and 400 miles, I've come to appreciate some of my equipment and curse some. I've found I need to carry:

Walking stick—Mine is homemade from a length of bamboo. It's light, strong and has saved me from doing "face plants" on the rocks countless times.

Bandanna—Many uses, from headgear to gripping hot cups and pots. Don't take to the trail without one.

Water filter—Many through-hikers don't carry one, but they're rolling the dice with giardia and other waterborne bugs. The modern

At the Bear Rocks overlook near Slatington, Pennsylvania, Don Hopey revels in the late-afternoon sunlight. Photo by Bill Wade, Pittsburgh Post-Gazette

ones are lightweight and small. Easier to be safe than sorry.

Stove—It's a must for coffee and oatmeal in the morning and a cup of tea in the evening. The lightest and most widely used model on the trail is the Whisperlite, but ours was a bust. My old Coleman Peak 1, rushed in as a replacement, was much more dependable and had the added benefit of having a flame modulator that allowed us to simmer.

I could have lived without:

Compass—I know you should carry one and I did, but if you get lost on the AT you're just not paying attention. Never used it.

Razor—No one shaves on the trail, not even the women.

Raincoat—I carried one and used it in the evening to keep warm a couple of times, but no one hikes with one on because it makes you sweat and you get wet anyway. Better to just get soaked from the rain and put a dry shirt on when the cloudburst ends. ▲

DELAWARE WATER GAP, PENNSYLVANIA

On a plate already crowded with baked beans, potato salad, a hot dog and an ear of corn, I squeeze in a square of the pineapple-and-Mandarin-orange Jello made by Maryetta Bitzer of Stroudsburg. Jonny Lane (Squirrel Fight) samples the green-beans amandine served up by locals Sandy Rader and Nancy Gould. And end-to-ender Keith Dailey (Smooth) makes a second—or is it a third?—trip to the dessert table.

It is a summer Thursday and the Presbyterian Church of the Mountain's weekly dinner for hikers—one stop on the merry, movable feast of food and fellowship that is the Appalachian Trail—is in full swing. Under threatening skies, 30 long-distance hikers make grilled hot dogs, fried chicken, casseroles, pies, cakes, brownies and cookies disappear in a bolt of trail magic.

Gould, coauthor of the beans amandine, said she enjoyed the dinners because she liked to hear hikers tell trail stories. "We met a guy last year who was going for the record for most hugs on the trail. He was sweaty and everything, but he hugged us."

"This is a great gesture," said 21-year-old Diana Humple, a through-hiker known as Raven and a recent University of Virginia graduate. "I did crazy miles to get in here in time for the dinner, and it's wonderful."

Despite rocky terrain that gives boots and their wearers a hammering, many of the hikers at the dinner had stepped up their pace through the Keystone State just so they could

About 30 through-hikers sup at the Thursday night Presbyterian Church of the Mountain dinner in Delaware Water Gap, Pennsylvania. Squirrel Fight is among the diners (right). Photo by Bill Wade, Pittsburgh Post-Gazette

Rob Adamson (Rob of Loxley) of Sheffield, England, climbs a 900-foot-high barren wall of stone coming out of Lehigh Gap. The barren hillside and the surrounding area are the result of a century of unregulated emissions from local zinc-mining and smelting operations.
Photo by Bill Wade, Pittsburgh Post-Gazette

make the dinner. Others extended their stay in the church's hostel to worship at the food service. Bill and I trooped 36 miles in two and a half days, then dropped anchor.

We began the last week of our six-week, 453-mile trek along the trail with a steep climb out of Lehigh Gap. We negotiated the barren, boulder-strewn face of a hill shaved clean of vegetation by a century of unregulated emissions from a zinc-mining-and-smelting operation along the Lehigh River.

The area, now a federal Superfund cleanup site where re-greening remains mostly a good thought, is a favorite of hikers because of its resemblance to the Dakota Badlands. It requires several rock scrambles and hand-hold climbs to get to the top, but the view of

Warren Doyle pauses in the backyard of the Presbyterian Church of the Mountain with the group of 14 through-hikers he is leading on the trail. Doyle, a professor of Appalachian studies at George Mason University in Virginia and a devotee of minimalist hiking, has hiked the trail 10 times. Photo by Bill Wade, Pittsburgh Post-Gazette

the valley and the meandering river and towns along its banks is as sweeping as any you're likely to find in the state.

On the ridge we caught up with through-hiker Rob Adamson (Rob of Loxley) of Sheffield, England, who, despite some protestations, agreed to hike off the trail to a Fourth of July party with us at the Blue Mountain Dome home of John Stempa and Linda Gellock, hikers and trail maintainers in the Smith Gap area.

Although the Brit insisted that black was the proper color for the occasion, red, white and blue was the clear crowd favorite as a half-dozen hikers mixed with the Stempa and Gellock families and friends. Stempa's mother Gladas posed for pictures with the hikers, taking her position in front of the camera after asking, "Which one of you smells best?"

"My reception here has been great," Rob said, "both from other hikers and from locals. The locals especially have been tolerant and generous. When hikers come in hot and smelly it would be easy for them to say get on your bike, but they don't. I think they like to know that people are taking an effort on the trail."

Our abbreviated week of hiking ended when we dropped off the Kittatinny Ridge, where the leafy canopy is mostly oak, poplars and maples, and descended into a dark hemlock forest. A well-worn, rocky path took us past waxy-green rhododendron thickets still brightened by delicate white blooms. Eventually the traffic noise from the toll bridge over the Delaware River rose to greet us.

After the sole-searing rock gauntlet along the Blue and Kittatinny ridges, the Church of the Mountain's dinner and hostel are welcome stops. There is food there for both the body and the soul.

Warren Doyle was easy to spot among the

John Stempa takes a photo of his mother, Gladas Stempa, and some of the through-hikers who stopped by the mountain dome home he shares with his wife, Linda Gellock. Avid hikers themselves, John and Linda, who live a mile off the trail near Smith Gap, have invited the day's passing of hikers to their family Fourth of July party. Rob of Loxley, in the red shirt (second from the right), is among the guests. Photo by Bill Wade, Pittsburgh Post-Gazette

dozen hikers who strolled off the trail and set up camp in the church's backyard. He was the trail icon wearing two different running shoes.

Doyle, who held the through-hike speed record of 66.3 days in 1973, has in recent years gained greater recognition for his minimalist hiking philosophy and group hikes. Before his last group hike in 1990, he went to a thrift shop and bought six pairs of sneakers for $1 a pair. He used only three on that hike. The others he saved for this one.

"I believe walking the trail is a countercul-

ture statement. It's one of the last bastions where people can learn to become free again," said the 44-year-old professor of Appalachian studies at George Mason University in Virginia, who was in the middle of his 10th 2,000-mile walk.

The hikers who make up this year's group, ranging in age from 25 to 62, started out on Springer Mountain in Georgia on April 29, and they're all still hiking. They expect to finish in 127 days and walk 16 to 18 miles a day, depending on each section's "difficulty, scenery and fun," Doyle said. A van carries the hikers' equipment from campsite to campsite nearly every day so hikers are free of the limitations of carrying 45- to 50-pound packs, except in sections of the Smokies in New Hampshire and all of Maine's 100-mile wilderness. "I try to spend at least two weeks a year on the trail, and this serves my purpose. It's like going to church—a higher love," Doyle said. "It's healthy, and every day I'm still learning, still enjoying."

John Mauro, a ridge runner from Auburn, Maine, has patrolled a 42-mile section of the trail from the Delaware Water Gap to just south of Lehigh Gap for six weeks and has made it to five of the Thursday dinners.

"There's always enough food. They always make the hikers go first and everyone is so nice," said Mauro, the youngest of 11 ridge runners employed by the Appalachian Trail Conference, various local hiking clubs and federal and state agencies. Their job is to educate hikers about low-

impact hiking and camping techniques, especially in heavy-use areas from Georgia to Maine.

"I'm tickled, on a high," Mauro said. "I feel a real, raw beauty here. The church folks go and do this and everyone is walking away with a big smile. It takes a special community to do this."

Pastor Karen Nickel, by virtue of her position already closer to God than most of the so-called "trail angels" we've met, said the church was struggling 20 years ago when it went looking for its mission. It found one in the steady stream of hikers passing less than a block from its front doors.

"We had a student pastor then who started feeding the hikers, and the ministry has just grown over the years," Nickel said. "We practice the spiritual discipline of hospitality, and the congregation has really learned to accept people as they are. Of course we realized quickly that what they needed most was a shower."

The Appalachian Trail Hikers Center in the church basement provides that hot shower—plus six bunks, a bathroom, a common room with overstuffed couches and chairs, and free Coleman fuel. Camping for overflow hikers is allowed on the lawn behind the church. The services Nickel provides are unadvertised.

In the three days we hung around the hostel, she took one hiker to the hospital for knee X rays, called a doctor for another who had stomach problems, hunted a bag of ice for a third who was nursing a groin pull and carted a carload to a mall movie. (We saw *Batman Forever* because *Apollo 13* was sold out.) She also told one would-be hiker, in no uncertain terms, that his loud, drunken behavior of the night before had made him unwelcome and he should plan on leaving immediately, if not sooner.

Andy McClain (Papa Bear) and his wife, Jan McClain (Honey), of Pittsburgh, stop on the I-80 bridge over the Delaware River, which carries hikers from Pennsylvania to New Jersey. The McClains are part of Warren Doyle's hiking group this summer and have been practicing for the hike with Doyle for three years.
Photo by Bill Wade, Pittsburgh Post-Gazette

Leaving Pennsylvania behind, Red Fox and Doc Vapor cross the I-80 bridge over the Delaware River and into New Jersey. Photo by Bill Wade, Pittsburgh Post-Gazette

"This is a place where a lot of hikers take two or three days off because the Pennsylvania rocks are really tough on them," Nickel said. "Sometimes they lose their nerve here. We try to be here for them."

Later, Mauro would write of the hiker dinner in the hostel's hiker register, noting that it was "sorta magical. I mean someone turned water into wine and provided loads of food. It was an intense event."

Neither the intensity nor the magic was diminished by the big, fat raindrops that began to splatter down as hikers helped church members clear, fold and put away the banquet tables.

▲ **Trail Mix —**
After a particularly brutal 18-mile scramble over sharp rocks between Smith Gap and the Kirkridge shelter, just a day out of the Delaware Water Gap, Bill Wade dragged into camp near dark, a good 45 minutes after everyone else. A gimpy knee, twisted a couple of days before, and large blisters on one heel had made his going slow. When he finally arrived, tired, sweaty and in obvious discomfort, I asked him, "Bill, what's hurting worse, the knee or the heel?" "The kneel," he misspoke accurately. ▲

A maple leaf sits on the branches of a small hemlock as the first signs of autumn's approach begin to mark the trail in New Hampshire. Photo by Michael Kodas, The Hartford Courant

CHAPTER 5

SUMMER TALES

JULY 5 – AUGUST 30, 1995

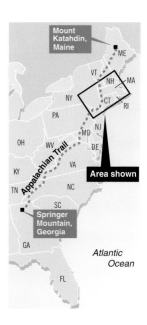

GREENWOOD LAKE, NEW YORK

**Text by
Steve Grant**

**Photography by
Michael Kodas**

All along the trail hikers are warned to store their food carefully at night. Bears love easy pickings.

But we weren't quick enough for a female of about 250 pounds that we came to know as Sophie.

Photographer Michael Kodas and I have begun our leg of the Appalachian Adventure, spending our first week walking north through New Jersey. We hiked from the Delaware Water Gap, on the Pennsylvania line, to this lakeside village a few miles into New York. Sophie welcomed us to the Garden State, which kept our attention with the unexpected all week.

Sophie, a two-year-old black bear weighing between 250 and 300 pounds, makes her way through Backpacker Campsite Number Two in the Delaware Water Gap National Recreation Area in New Jersey after attempting to steal Steve Grant's backpack. The collar around Sophie's neck monitors her movements for New Jersey wildlife officials. Photo by Michael Kodas, The Hartford Courant

On our first day out, we arrived at a camp-site on Kittatinny Ridge at about 7 P.M. There, David W. Simpson, a trail worker who keeps order during the busy summer months, advised us that there had been bear sightings.

We had just dropped our packs when someone about 100 yards south shouted, "Bear." We grabbed our cameras and ran—to get photos—Simpson running with us. But the bear bounded off with deceptive speed, headed west.

"Sometimes she circles around," Simpson said. I realized that circling would bring the bear through our campsite. I ran back.

We found Sophie dragging my 47-pound backpack into the woods, tearing at the top with her teeth to get at the food inside. We had planned to hang our food from a tree each night to protect it from animals.

Unlike its western cousin, the grizzly—which can be dangerous when confronted—the black bear of the East is a timid bear, and usually runs when it sees people. Food complicates things, but even after snatching a hiker's pantry, a black bear can usually be scared off.

We chased her, shouting phrases she undoubtedly could not understand, such as

After finishing a day of hiking, Steve Grant and Mike Kodas watch the sun set over the High Point State Park war monument, which marks the highest point in the state as well as our starting point on the trail. Photo by Michael Kodas, The Hartford Courant

"Drop it, Sophie" and "Let go." We shot photographs the whole time.

Finally, Sophie dropped the pack and bounded away. There were three large tears in the pack fabric, dripping with bear saliva. My reading glasses, still in their leather case, had been the centerpiece of one bite and were mangled. What mattered most to us at the moment, the food, was unscathed.

"She didn't really want a confrontation," Simpson said. In fact, she had not once seemed hostile during the incident. Rather, she seemed confused, and I felt uncomfortable knowing I had shooed her from a piece of land that she had more claim to than I did. On the other hand, I didn't feel she had a right to my dinner.

The next day one of Simpson's colleagues, Gary F. Schmitt, told us there are several hundred bears in New Jersey. The bear popula-

Bear Mountain Bridge, spanning the Hudson River, connects Bear Mountain State Park (to the right of the river) to the mountain called Anthony's Nose. Anthony's Nose was a popular subject with painters in the Hudson River School, who traveled from New York to paint landscapes of the mountain in the mid-1800s. Photo by Michael Kodas, The Hartford Courant

tion is growing in the East as its forests, often cut over until earlier this century, become more mature and can provide habitats.

"I've been seeing a lot of bears with two or three cubs, twins and triplets," Schmitt said. He had given Sophie her name. Sophie, he said, was born where I met her, on a rocky ridge covered with chestnut oaks and blueberry bushes.

The trail through New Jersey is a pleasant walk, less challenging than some of the more mountainous sections, but still difficult in places and prettier than many people realize. The trail for many miles is wooded and

rocky—so rocky that each step means a decision about where to place your foot. Elsewhere the trail follows old, grass-covered roads in the woods or skirts the edges of farm fields. It bumps into the swing sets and pools of suburbia in places and gets itself tossed onto paved roads in others.

John C. Chanas of Stillwater, New Jersey, was hiking with friends and family atop 1,653-foot Sunrise Mountain one afternoon. "Put in a good word for New Jersey," he said. "It is not as bad as most people make it out to be." As he spoke, rain clouds were lifting, giving way to sun, and all that could be seen for miles to the east and west were woods and farms. The New Jersey Turnpike, from which many people have drawn their smoke-stack image of the state, was nowhere in sight.

What we found in New Jersey was a trail in midsummer lushness. Rhododendrons had either peaked or were just beginning to fade. Summer wildflowers were in full bloom, even some of the goldenrods that would become more abundant as the summer waned. Blue-berries were rarely more than an arm's length away, and they were beginning to ripen. Early in the morning the ripe berries were cool, chilled by the night air. By midafternoon, ridgetop berries were hot, a mouthful tasting almost like a piece of blueberry pie straight from the oven, if you didn't mind imagining the rest of the pie.

One of the virtues of long-distance hiking is that it reduces life to the essentials, like food, and lets you ponder them, or anything else, as you trudge mile after mile, your mind free to make whatever associations it will.

Over the course of a morning, as energy is burned up, the pace slows. Feet that strode with authority now seem encumbered, stum-bling over little rocks that an hour before passed under uneventfully. It is then that the power of a piece of fruit or a hunk of bread and a bite of cheese is driven home. Within minutes of eating—the fuel begins burning—as dramatic as tossing another log on the fire.

Late one afternoon, hungry and tired, a through-hiker named Rebecca Clark of Windham, Maine, plunked down on the trail and cooked a pasta dinner on her trail stove, eating it from the pot as others walked by.

"If I start feeling tired or grumpy, even if there is a good reason for me to feel that way, if I stop and eat something and drink some water, I feel great," she said.

We have kept our meals simple, and they include some commercially prepared freeze-dried entrées. But I've prepared some light-weight trail meals of my own, too. I've brought along two different kinds of tomato sauces, which were dried in a home dehydra-

A timber rattlesnake, which sent Michael Kodas leaping from a boulder earlier in the morning, enjoys a late breakfast. Photo by Michael Kodas, The Hartford Courant

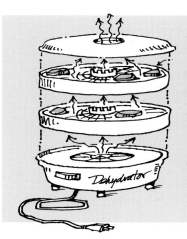

DEHYDRATOR

◆ Dried foods are a staple of backpacking meals. They can be bought or made at home, using a dehydrator, a simple device in which fresh foods, such as apple slices, are placed on lattice-work trays that are stacked one atop the other. In this exploded view, a fan blows warm air through the trays, drying the food in a matter of hours. The food is then packaged for later use.

PHIL LOHMAN / The Hartford Courant

tor, and a pesto sauce of basil, garlic, nuts and olive oil that's been reduced in the same way, so that each sauce is only a fraction of its former weight. I also brought home-dried apple slices and several home-prepared campfire bread mixes.

One of the camp breads, called a bannock, combines oat and whole-wheat flours. I've often made bannock in a frying pan over a wood fire, but fires are prohibited on many sections of the trail, so I attempted to bake it in an aluminum pot over a tiny gas backpacking stove, which, unfortunately, was hard to regulate. The heat was too high and the bread got scorched, but we ate it anyway.

Late in the week, after hiking from a campsite near High Point Monument, the highest point in New Jersey at 1,803 feet, we reached the summit of Pochuck Mountain, about 14 miles away. Under a canopy of hemlock trees, we camped and made a dinner of home-dried marinara sauce over fettuccine noodles, served with Parmesan cheese, and drank from our ever-present water bottles. The dehydrated sauce renewed itself gracefully as we added water and left it to simmer. In a quiet forest, as the sun set, the food was simple and special. We made coffee and walked to an overlook to photograph the sunset. Over a green horizon of succeeding ridgetops we could see the monument where we had started the day. Above were ribbons of salmon-colored sky, with a bit of the sun, muted by clouds, barely visible.

Through-hikers John Bevans (Jones), Matt Bahis (Anteater), Christian Reitmeier (Grover) and Jonny Lake (Squirrel Fight) meet Father Mark O'Connor after mass at the Graymoor Friary. The friary, located near the trail, has a tradition of extending hospitality to hikers. Photo by Michael Kodas, The Hartford Courant

Another few days of sun and all the blue-berries will be ripe. Then Sophie won't be seen much in the campsites atop Kittatinny Ridge. Her diet will be simple yet rich.

"When the berries are really ripe," Simpson said, "the bears are not as much of a problem."

POUGHQUAG, NEW YORK

On a clear day you can see Manhattan from some of the ridgetops along the trail through New York state, but we never saw the city. The smog was too much, and, besides, the hiking was so uncomfortable—painful, almost—that we spent only moments on rocky, sunscorched outlooks.

We were hiking through a heat wave that presented the trail in one of its unforgiving extremes. Along with the heat there also were reminders of Benton MacKaye, the Connecticut-born planner who proposed the trail in 1921, envisioning it as a footpath that could foster a modest, almost utopian, rural society.

The ridges that carry the trail, he said, could serve as natural buffers to help contain the sprawl that few others worried about back then. Ideally, the trail would be a refuge for the harried people of eastern cities, New York among them.

It certainly was a refuge for many hikers who, after a morning spent hiking up and over the summit of Bear Mountain, cruised down the other side and into Bear Mountain State Park, where thousands of people were coping with a 103° day.

The contrasts between trail culture and state park life were startling. After days in the woods, including a night in which a whippoorwill's insistent, persistent call was the loudest sound we heard, we were struck by noise. After days of hiking single file and seeing perhaps 30 people all day, we now encountered people hiking six- or eight-abreast, as far as we could see.

The trail, concrete in places, blacktop in

Anteater, Jones, Grover and Squirrel Fight pray during mass at the Graymoor Friary just east of the Hudson River in New York. Photo by Michael Kodas, The Hartford Courant

others, passes through the picnic area and by a massive swimming pool, perhaps 60 feet from the trail. The trail continues through the Trailside Museum, which includes a zoo in which bears and other animals are housed. Here at the zoo is the lowest point on the Appalachian Trail, elevation 124 feet.

Tanner Critz (Wayah) of Atlanta, Georgia, dives into Canopus Lake in New York next to Route 301. Several other hikers sit on a boulder in the lake while cooling off during a heat wave that sent temperatures into the 100° range for several days straight. Photo by Michael Kodas, The Hartford Courant

MacKaye saw his trail as a place where a walker would have "a chance to catch a breath, to study the dynamic forms of nature and the possibilities of shifting to them the burdens now carried on the backs of men." That statement hints at his broader goal, now largely forgotten and unrealized.

MacKaye hoped the trail could become the foundation of a series of camps, where people from cities—factory workers, notably—could refresh themselves in nature. In time, he thought, the trail might include nonprofit forestry and farm camps, where people from cities might find rewarding work with timber and crops in a pleasant rural atmosphere, one he feared was disappearing.

"Most people associate MacKaye with the footpath," says Charles H. W. Foster, an adjunct faculty member at the John F. Kennedy School of Government at Harvard University and an author and consultant on natural resources. "That footpath was a means to an end."

Perhaps the zoo, nature museum and the picnic area at Bear Mountain fit in with MacKaye's idea for recreation camps. The boomboxes, it seemed to me, would not.

The trail in New York is a rapid succession of modest but often steep peaks mantled in a mostly hardwood forest dominated by oaks. From almost any vantage point spreads a view of other mountains, including the Catskills and the Taconics. But, as in New Jersey and parts of other states, suburbia laps up against the trail.

While passing through New Jersey, we appreciated the brooks and streams that invariably flow in the valleys between the ridges of the Appalachians. One of the most pleasant sounds of a woodland walk is the gurgle and hiss of a stream announcing itself. By the time we hit New York, however, months of dry weather and the heat had largely quieted that voice.

Lakes, always inviting, became even more precious than usual. In Harriman State Park late one day, we noticed Island Lake a few hundred yards off the trail. We walked over. From some large rocks, three young men were diving. On another rock were a father and his children. Elsewhere we saw nothing but trees and water, and a deer feeding on the far shore. We stripped to our hiking shorts and dived in. I found a shallow, sandy spot and lay there for 10 minutes, motionless, only my head above water.

SALISBURY, CONNECTICUT

Benton MacKaye once said that the point of the trail was to see, to really see.

Allison, my 12-year-old daughter, joined me for three days on the trail last week, beginning in New York and continuing to Kent, about 25 miles south of here. She saw something I didn't.

Late one hot afternoon we stopped for a lemonade break, then continued on, refreshed. Moments later, we came upon a log bridge over a stream that flowed, cool and clear, through a shady forest thick with deep-green hemlocks and their soft carpet of needles. The trail guide said it was Duell Hollow Brook.

"Dad, can we stop?" she asked.

I mentioned that five minutes before we had taken a 20-minute break, that we had several miles to go before we would reach camp, that it was already 4:30. It didn't make sense to stop. But, somehow, I realized that it did.

It was for moments like this that people hike the Appalachian Trail.

"Sure," I said.

We took off our boots and socks and waded in. The water felt refreshing to feet

Patricia Alexander (Saprophyte, left) of Virginia Beach, Virginia, and Diana Humple (Raven), of Vienna, Virginia, rest along the Palisades Parkway between Harriman and Bear Mountain state parks in New York while night-hiking to avoid the 100-plus-° daytime temperatures. After swimming all day in Lake Tiorati, they started hiking after 7 P.M. when the heat broke, and hiked until after midnight. Photo by Michael Kodas, The Hartford Courant

Through-hiker Squirrel Fight struggles through "The Lemon Squeezer," a tight crevice in Harriman State Park, New York. Photo by Michael Kodas, The Hartford Courant

well on their way to being sore. I found a pool deep enough to submerge myself in. Allison looked for minnows. Then we sat side by side on a flat rock, our feet in the stream, talking quietly in the quiet woods, the only other sound the riffles of the brook. Shafts of late-afternoon sun pierced through hemlock boughs.

We got to camp soon enough.

Hikers are drawn to the trail by places like Duell Hollow Brook, a piece of America away from the din. But the din is never far away—we often hear trucks, cars or machines off in the distance—and the noise even makes its way to the trail sometimes.

Only a few years ago, the idea of hikers with telephones in their backpacks was science fiction. Now it is a reality; we've already encountered one hiker talking on the telephone from the summit of a mountain. We've also noticed hikers carrying tiny radios with headphones, and we've been told that miniature, battery-powered televisions have shown up in some campsites, as have new devices that use satellite technology to pinpoint a hiker's location in the event of injury.

Some of these high-tech devices, however—the phones and the TVs notably—get the same reception from hikers as a swarm of mosquitoes. They're an issue along the trail, even among hikers who didn't hesitate to trade their old canvas backpacks for space-age, lightweight synthetics.

"I'm a computer programmer; I come out here to get away from that stuff," said through-hiker Bill Cleveland (Doc Vapor) of Atlanta. "I think most people are out here to step aside from technology." Even if civilization is never far from the trail, many of the hikers want at least the illusion of wilderness or, at a minimum, a trail without sitcoms or telephone chitchat. What they want are the sights, sounds and smells of nature, without the clutter of everyday life.

Cleveland and many others seem to draw the line at the point where high-tech affects someone else—if a cellular phone can be seen or heard, for example. "As long as the person is not bothering somebody else, I don't care," he says.

Over the past week, we completed the section of the trail that runs through New York and hiked much of Connecticut, finding that the trail is a little wilder and more remote there.

An entry from the register at the shrine adjacent to the trail on the Graymoor Friary's property. Photo by Michael Kodas, The Hartford Courant

Trail maintenance volunteers build low, stone dams to divert water and to prevent erosion on steep parts of the trail. Illustration by Phil Lohman.

Almost out of water, we stopped by a brook on Sharon Mountain only to find it dry. Adam B. Cole, an Appalachian Mountain Club ridge runner, happened by. His job was to help keep order on the trail during the busiest months. He was awaiting a new cellular phone, which he viewed as a valuable tool in the event of an emergency, or for alerting other trail crew workers to potential problems with hikers or trail conditions. "I carried one last week, and I felt like I was doing my job better," he said.

Inevitably, the trail culture reflects our broader society, and technology will continue to change life there too. Michael and I, incidentally, do not have a cellular phone, TV or radio along.

The trail changes in another way, as well. It changes physically from year to year, as the route is altered to improve a view, dodge

Steve Grant pours some cool water over the feet of his daughter Allison, while they take a break at Duell Hollow Brook in New York, where the Appalachian Trail crosses into Connecticut. The younger Grant joined her father for a couple of days and 22 miles of hiking. Photo by Michael Kodas, The Hartford Courant

some new development or protect a sensitive piece of woodland habitat.

The Connecticut section of the trail has been one of the most controversial routes since MacKaye proposed it in 1921. No sooner had MacKaye suggested the trail than there were alternate suggestions to route it mostly through New York, almost avoiding Connecticut entirely.

Within Connecticut, there was disagreement over the route, some people favoring a route west of the Housatonic River, others a route east of the river. A farmer and school-bus driver from Sherman, Ned Anderson, resolved the issue by cutting the trail himself, following the easterly route.

Fifty years later, when the U.S. government came in to buy a permanent route for the trail, the issue resurfaced. Property owners along the existing route were reluctant to have a permanent route through or near their land.

With fewer property owners to deal with and sizable amounts of publicly owned land available, the National Park Service chose the route west of the Housatonic—and the trail, a decade ago, jumped across the river. Finally, the trail was back where some people had wanted it 70 years earlier.

The new trail was plotted by Norman Sills, a retired Salisbury farmer. It is a more remote route than the previous one, but it also sacrifices some interesting landscapes, including some striking views from Mohawk Mountain.

The land Sills farmed for many years,

The license plate on Blaise Desivour's truck shows his devotion to the trail. Photo by Michael Kodas, The Hartford Courant

adjacent to the trail, is well known among trail devotees because it includes Rand's View, a vantage point that is quintessential New England and was part of the trail then and now. From the edge of the woods a pastoral foreground, framed by the trees, slopes away. From behind and to the left rises a chain of imposing, well-defined peaks, beginning with Bear Mountain in Salisbury. On a very clear day, Mount Greylock in Massachusetts, 50 miles away, can be seen.

After a steep climb up Prospect Mountain, I saw the sign for Rand's View, which was a few hundred feet from the trail, down a side path. It would have been easy to pass by, avoid the extra steps and save some time. But I walked down and sat, taking in the view.

Allison had gone home by then, but she helped me to see.

TOP: *Leslie Clapp (Flower Power) of Blue Hill, Maine, hikes out of the Silver Hill Campsite in Kent, Connecticut.* Photo by Michael Kodas, The Hartford Courant

BOTTOM: *David Heinstadt (Red Fox), of Towson, Maryland, hangs his water bag from a fallen tree to make a shower at the Silver Hill Campsite, where he is taking a "zero-mile day" to bathe, do his laundry and relax.* Photo by Michael Kodas, The Hartford Courant

BECKET, MASSACHUSETTS

We met at one of those points where the trail narrows to a body width, near Bear Mountain in Salisbury, Connecticut. They were headed south; I was northbound.

Walking alone, I was slipping into a woodland reverie, pleased that I managed to notice that the forest was changing, the bronzy bark of yellow birch showing up more often, along with smooth-barked beeches and white birches. This forest hinted of Vermont to come. The oak-dominated woods of New Jersey, New York and parts of Connecticut, pretty themselves, were largely behind us.

I had been frustrated because I couldn't pay enough attention to these surroundings, to the birds, trees, insects and wildflowers, and still make sufficient progress in our hike. Wasn't the whole point of backpacking to commune with nature? Maybe it was better to walk into the woods unencumbered, find a stump to sit on and soak up the sights, sounds and smells. Did we need to spend all day clambering over rocks and roots, muscles taxed, struggling to reach a campsite where setting up tents, making supper and cleaning up consumed what was left of daylight, and me?

Flower Power and Steve Lund (Uncle Wolf) of Boulder, Colorado, cross the Housatonic River in Kent, Connecticut, in the early morning after camping the night before on a small island in the river. Photo by Michael Kodas, The Hartford Courant

But my thoughts were interrupted. In front of me stood the Mountain Marching Mamas, five women, walking single file. They were smiling.

We introduced ourselves, chatting long enough for me to realize that I had better get out my notebook. The youngest of the five was days from her 50th birthday; three of them were grandmothers. They agreed among themselves to make our conversation their hourly break, took off their packs and sat down.

Bunny Schneider (Mother Superior) of Bradenton, Florida, told me the group had been hiking sections of the trail since 1978, usually for about two weeks a year. She said they expected to finish the trail in about two years.

"We're slow, but we're steady," she said.

Slow was 8 to 15 miles a day—not unlike what Michael and I had been doing. I

Light bleeds through the woods surrounding the Belter Campsite in Sharon, Connecticut, after an early morning storm. Photo by Michael Kodas, The Hartford Courant

exceeded 15 miles only once, after being on the trail for a month.

These women were a sharp contrast to the backpackers we so often meet, many of them college-age people so unfettered that they have no plans beyond the next bend in the trail. For them, if my experience is any guide, life on the trail is not all that different from life away from the trail. Often the bed they make in a three-sided shelter is only a measure more rustic than the one they left in some college-town apartment. But for those of us who have become fussy about our coffee, the trail is a sharp departure from the everyday world.

What were we doing out here, especially if

there wasn't time to poke about among the wildflowers? Did this make any sense?

The Mountain Marching Mamas had answers. Each of them, long ago, had discovered for herself what was valuable about a stint in the woods, and they keep coming back.

Ellen Kilpatrick (Mama Kazoo) of Gainesville, Florida, calls the trail to mind when things are difficult back home. "When the going gets tough, I just visualize something on the trail I thought I couldn't do, but did," she said.

"It puts everything in perspective," said Mary Pfennig (Hoosier Mama) of Rising Sun, Indiana. "I require a lot less when I go home.

You don't need TV and air-conditioning. You can get by with so much less."

"Possessions are weight," added Sylvia Crump (Orange Blossom) of De Leon Springs, Florida. "I don't buy knickknacks anymore. I don't even go into the gift shops."

"It rejuvenates me, it fills me up again, it's a spiritual experience," said Charme Burns (Gypsy) of Gainesville. "At the end of the hike I feel like I am ready to go back to my family life and my job and give them my best again."

Their packs were light, as light as 19 pounds, far lighter than the pack I was carrying. And though they did not fit the mold of the stereotypical hiker, they were as comfortable in the woods as anyone we had met.

Nearing the end of a month on the trail, we, too, are feeling comfortable. I've lost weight—10 pounds easily—and the pain I felt every night during the first week has disappeared. We notice now that we climb surely over mountains that a few weeks ago took a heavy toll. We don't huff and puff the way we did.

It is a wonderful, satisfying feeling, a gift of the trail and a reminder that our bodies want to be used, must be used. Western civilization has evolved into a postindustrial tangle of offices, but it left our bodies behind. They still think we need to work the land all day.

We are often dirty, but even the dirt seems healthy. This is not the dirt that turns a facecloth gray after a day in the city. This is soil and leaves and moss and bark, and we are almost proud to wear it on the back of our calves. We are not so proud of it, however, that we don't wash it off whenever we can.

After leaving the Mountain Marching Mamas, I hiked into Massachusetts, reaching an area known as Sages Ravine at midday. Sages Ravine Brook is a beautiful, cold, tumbling mountain stream that is punctuated with big, dark pools of clear water.

Rand's View on Prospect Mountain in Salisbury, Connecticut, shows the mountains of northern Connecticut, the Berkshires of Massachusetts and Mount Greylock in northern Massachusetts. The vista shows northbound hikers the mountains that will test them for the next week or so of hiking. Photo by Michael Kodas, The Hartford Courant

I stopped and thought about taking a dip, but decided against it because it had begun to rain. Here was the first of what would be five thunderstorms over a period of four days, thunderstorms that made the trail slippery and dangerous in places and triggered mosquito hatches.

But the ravine was too beautiful to pass by. I splashed water from the brook on my face and sat on a log bridge over the brook as the rain dappled the water. I drank some, after filtering it, though I thought the brook didn't deserve such treatment.

Nearby a group of young teens and their leader rested. The blank faces of some of them told me that the satisfactions of hiking had eluded them. They were still wondering why people do this. The trail, I sensed, held no meaning for them. It would have to come to them.

For the Mountain Marching Mamas, the trail is rich and pleasant. When we parted, they did what they often do as they walk: They sang.

It was "Happy trails to you. . ." that faded away as we hiked off in different directions.

GLASTENBURY MOUNTAIN, VERMONT

Text by Susan Campbell

Illustrations by Phil Lohman

I am hurling curses to what feels like a fall wind all the way up the old fire tower on Glastenbury Mountain in southern Vermont. I have hiked for hours through mist and cold rain without enough warm clothing. When Michael suggests that we climb the tower for a better view, I tell him I can see the mist fine from where I am.

But I remove my pack and climb anyway. I am here to see the ghost town of Glastenbury because the notion of a ghost town in the crowded East—where nearly every parcel of land has been claimed and named—intrigues me. The driving mist stings as I climb and peer down through the pines.

Bunny Schneider, of Bradenton, Florida, combs her hair on Bear Mountain in Salisbury, Connecticut, during a break from her hiking with the Mountain Marching Mamas. Schneider's mirror shows the logo of the "Mamas." Photo by Michael Kodas, The Hartford Courant

Ellen Kilpatrick of Gainesville, Florida, leads other members of the Mountain Marching Mamas on the trail. The women take turns as leader of the group, share everything and even count the planks on the floor of each shelter they stay in and divide the total by five to determine how much sleeping space they each get. They rarely get together between hikes. Photo by Michael Kodas, The Hartford Courant

Doug Forrester, of Glasgow, Scotland, and James Goldsbrough, of Chesterfield, England, both counselors at Camp Slaone in Sharon, Connecticut, bathe in the dawn as they watch the sun rise from their sleeping bags in the Riga lean-to in Salisbury, Connecticut. Many of the counselors at the camp, who are from England and Scotland, take advantage of the opportunity to work in a U.S. camp to earn money for travel around the country. Photo by Michael Kodas, The Hartford Courant

From above, the mist looks like white horses running through the trees.

Later, hiking down the mountain on the soft pine needles, the wind quiets and the mist settles like cobwebs on either side of the trail. We slip through—ghosts ourselves—past depressions of old foundations near the former Glastenbury Railroad, Mining and Manufacturing Company. If you are looking for ghosts, this is the perfect day.

There is a lot of time to think out here, and the mist and quiet are perfect conduits. There are no vistas to distract, and our bantering fades. There is only thought.

The small Massachusetts towns we have passed through—Dalton and Cheshire and North Adams, where we set up shop in a Pizza Hut while a driving rain filled potholes—seem so far away.

After leaving Dalton we hiked up and over Crystal Mountain to St. Mary of the Assumption Church in Cheshire, Massachusetts, the local hiker hostel that housed 400 hikers last year. Father Tom Begley (Father Time), a part-time hiker, has only a few miles to go to complete the entire trail. He's been here for 10 years, and members of the parish gathered in the hall for church suppers are accustomed to hiker stench—a mix of dirt, dried sweat, wet boots and mildewed clothing.

A few times, I have bent to snap the waist belt of my backpack and prayed, "Dear God, let that be my boots, and not me, that I'm smelling." That was early on. I don't care as much anymore.

Later we hiked up Mount Greylock, at 3,491 feet the highest point in Massachusetts, amid thunder that sounded as if it was six inches above our heads. It was a warm rain, though. I'm told it's a nice view from there, but I never saw through the fog.

We're all out here for something: the fresh air, avoiding the job market, seeing if we still have the legs for it, rebuilding our marriage, on a goof.

And if you're out here not particularly looking for anything, like computer whiz John Albrecht (Sans Souci), of Mantua, Ohio, it will probably find you. Albrecht is 40, and when he told the folks at his old job that he was leaving to pursue his lifelong dream of hiking the trail, they asked him when he was going to get the red convertible, too.

"This is not a midlife crisis," Albrecht says. "What's a midlife crisis?"

Beats me. I spent my first night in the Kay Wood shelter 16 miles from where I started at Becket Mountain, off to one side, trying not to ignite everyone's tent with my Whisperlite stove. A few days later, I was diving into the jokes and shared food with people I'd just met. The three-sided rustic shelters can be hellish, sleeping between the snorer and the tooth-grinder, or they can be a fantastic grown-up sleep-over without the sex.

It's the little things out here—a successful round of hula-hooping, a shared carrot snack, a particularly brave chipmunk attacking a pack, a sip of water when you're low—that make life rich. No matter what, no matter who, you have it good. I met Cindy Chandler of Dalton, Massachusetts, on a rocky climb in northern Massachusetts. She was section-hiking through Massachusetts and Connecticut with her seven children—one of whom she had sent home to go to a birthday party. Life could be loads harder.

The trails north from the Kay Wood shelter are alternately muddy and rocky. Some sections look as if a giant child threw blocks

down a hill, and those are your foot- and handholds. In dry weather, the climb is grinding. In wet, it's maddening.

But in Glastenbury, the soft pine needles on the trail leave us free to contemplate a mystery that started with the Mahicans, an eastern Algonquin tribe that would not settle where the four winds meet and claimed only the valleys.

The tribe was pushed west by Europeans who claimed the higher land as well, creating a teeming coal town with a bandstand where local musicians played straight through Saturday night, stopping just in time for the organist to make it to the church for services. Still, an active social life couldn't keep the townspeople when the coal ran out. A few more energetic residents collected ferns from the surrounding forests to send to New York City florists, but there was only so much to be made on greenery.

In 1937, by special act of the Vermont Leg-

Students in a class from the Wilderness School in East Hartland, Connecticut, join hands while regaining their composure after weathering a severe thunderstorm on Mount Everett in southern Massachusetts. Photo by Michael Kodas, The Hartford Courant

islature, the town was officially unorganized. All that's left now are the depressions from old foundations and the stories of unexplained disappearances—such as that of Bennington College student Paula Welden in 1946, hunter Middie Rivers in 1945, and woodswoman Freida Langer in 1950. The mysteries moved one author to call the area the Bennington Triangle.

I am thinking about that. And I am thinking that I have sweated through my clothes, huffed up hills weak from hunger, watched my feet swell and shivered myself to sleep. I am having a hell of a good time.

KILLINGTON, VERMONT

The conversation was limping along, in part because Jonathan Curtis of Chapel Hill, North Carolina, was in that through-hiker state of mind where any discussion was worth jumping into with both feet. That, and the fact that the caretaker who'd wandered up to southern Vermont's Peru Peak shelter at twilight to collect $4 from each hiker just wasn't getting Curtis' jokes.

"Now, tell me again why I have to pay," said Curtis as he fished the bills from his hiker's wallet, a large Ziploc bag. The caretaker care-

Charles Ellis (Santa Clause), of Baltimore, reads a trail sign in Monterey, Massachusetts, that was downed, along with thousands of trees, by a spring tornado that severely damaged the Appalachian Trail and the communities of Monterey and Great Barrington. Ellis is finishing a hike he started in 1990 to raise money through pledges for the Salvation Army. Photo by Michael Kodas, The Hartford Courant

fully explained that that portion of the Appalachian Trail was heavily traveled, and the path's maintainers, the Green Mountain Club, hoped to regulate use by charging a toll. Those who didn't want to pay would stay in shelters or campsites at either end of the area around Stratton Pond, Vermont's most heavily used lake, thus spreading out the impact.

Vermont's wilderness is continually threatened by people who don't understand low-impact hiking and camping, he said, and the state's particular beauty must be preserved. Right about there, he lost Curtis.

"I suppose beatings would work the same, if you spread them out," Curtis said. The caretaker grabbed his belongings and quickly disappeared into the dark.

The discussion is the perfect meditation for this part of America's footpath, where Benton MacKaye's notion that the wilderness should be accessible to all is sorely tested, where today the wilderness is a little more civilized and sanitized than perhaps he had envisioned. Today, if MacKaye, father of the Appalachian Trail, climbed that tree on Stratton Mountain where he had seen visions of the trail, he'd see ski trails of Bromley cutting through his beloved woods, sunlight glistening off the windows of the condos at the faux-Bavarian Stratton Village and an ugly purple haze of pollution settling over the valleys of the Green Mountains.

The Appalachian Trail and the Long Trail, which runs together with the AT for part of Vermont, cut along a ridge that divides the Pico and Killington ski areas. All of Vermont's tallest peaks—including the four we passed this week—sport ski resorts. In summer, the lifts take vacationers to the peaks for rides down in everything from alpine slides to fancy go-karts and mountain bikes. The Pico-Killington corridor has been the subject of extensive lawsuits and discussions among

Four-year-old Tiffany Chandler, center, gets a drink from her mother, Cindy Chandler (Rain Princess) of Dalton, Massachusetts, during a rest break at Finerty Pond in Massachusetts. Photo by Michael Kodas, The Hartford Courant

environmentalists, trail groups, landowners, government officials and the ski-slope operators. It is a battle that continues.

Before Europeans arrived, Mahicans and Mohawks wanted the land, but neither would settle near the other's territory in the land between New York and south-central Vermont. Instead, they hunted those gray areas and moved farther apart to cut trees and burn stumps and plant elaborate gardens, which were the particular domain of the women. This time of year, the men would return from hunting for Green Corn Festival, during which they would harvest the crops and celebrate a native thanksgiving.

Around Stratton, there is broken glass along the trail, and farther north a caretaker warned me away from the Governor Clement shelter just off Robinson Brook because hikers had been awakened two nights earlier by a Honda Civic loaded with teenagers looking to sample a different kind of wild life. I never saw them.

Right after I was warned away, while on my way to bathe in a creek, I flushed a grouse. The helicopter sound of its leave-taking almost sent me up a tree.

I have only bathed in a brook twice now, and the notion that local townspeople might come calling made me move fairly quickly. But there is something about stripping down and lowering yourself into a brook at twilight that is natural and sensual and innocent all at once. I felt as if I was getting away with something, and I laughed out loud.

The same goes for drinking out of a spring. My water purifier is getting a workout, but occasionally there have been ice-cold springs you can drink straight. I laugh here, too. One hiker said he always trusts water out of a pipe, and when he was reminded that sewage flows through a pipe, he thought for a moment and said, "I'd drink that, too." I'm not there yet.

But I ate a piece of chicken sandwich dropped by Michael Kodas at the snack bar at Bromley, where we watched people shoot

Cindy Chandler ties the shoes of her daughter, Tiffany, on a bridge over Finerty Pond in western Massachusetts, while several other Chandler children wait to pass. Chandler and six of her children are hiking 100 miles from Vermont to Salisbury, Connecticut. All of the children wear boots and backpacks, although three of them are under the age of seven and one is still nursing. Photo by Michael Kodas, The Hartford Courant

down the hill in sporty Devalkarts, gravity-powered go-karts with fat yellow wheels. We got there by way of a chairlift. I ate that chicken to prove a point, but I can't remember what it was now.

I am learning to set up my campsite gently, and to do an idiot check when I'm through to make sure I don't leave anything behind. Even a careful hiker can threaten the trail. Erosion has forced rerouting along Northam Brook near Clarendon, and the trail coming off Pico is eroded knee-deep from rain and footsteps.

Not all ski-slope operators and environmentalists are at odds. Bromley lets hikers use its summit warming hut, a clean building that moved Greg Pflug (Johnny Reb) of Winter Park, Florida, to say, "If they put up a place like this in Florida, people would homestead it."

Bill Cairns, director of Bromley Resort operations, has hiked the trail extensively. He's also heli-skied off Baker Peak and Peru Peak.

Such an activity is hard to imagine, walking through the second-growth spruce of both peaks. Climbing up the last 100 feet of the granite summit of Baker Peak while the wind whipped me around, I felt as if I were climbing up on God's porch. It is not the height of the mountains here (Baker is 2,850 feet) that made me feel that way. It is the sheer magnitude of the views, the undulating wave after wave of green rolling off into infinity.

But you sometimes forget the view down among the natives. I walked through a pasture of Holsteins just north of the rocks worn smooth by water in Clarendon Gorge. I reached out to pet one to see if it was real. Before then, I'd only seen the black-and-white cows pictured on food products. She took off, bumped into another cow, and started a small

Mount Greylock, the inspiration for Herman Melville's Moby Dick *glows green through the window of the author's study at Arrowhead, the Melville home in Pittsfield, Massachusetts. The Appalachian Trail now climbs over Greylock, which looked like a huge white whale to the author when it was covered with snow.* Photo by Michael Kodas, The Hartford Courant

stampede. In the next pasture, a little self-consciously, I just waved.

But I was only a little self-conscious, as I was only a little sorry about trying to choke Michael. He'd been pushing for a long day to keep up with our schedule, so I agreed to 18 miles. With darkness closing in, I spent the last 2 miles vilifying him and his family, and when he passively said from behind, "What I hear you saying is that you're not having fun," I turned and reached for his neck. He blocked, and I only scratched him.

Hiking the trail takes its toll on even the most loosely joined of couples. One poignant entry in the Pico Camp register told us that a popular married couple had hiked this far north only to decide to get a divorce. "She is tired of my Southern ass," the man wrote. The stresses of making the mileage and working out mutual goals is hard enough off trail. On trail, it can be impossible. There are couples out here who are strengthening their vows, and those who are seeing that the shark ain't swimming.

I am over my distress of the 18-mile day. It's hardly even noteworthy, considering there are people who do 30-mile days. Truth to tell, big mileage hardly seems the point. On my longest day so far, I saw only a blurred green tunnel and, when he led and I kept up, the back of Michael's boots. I daresay there was more to be seen that day. I wouldn't know. I was too busy moving ahead, sticking to a schedule. I guess there's a metaphor in there somewhere.

Robert Tate (Danger Moose, right) garners applause for his skill with a hula hoop from a group of hikers at a Vermont shelter. Tate, a through-hiker from Cincinnati, hikes with the hula hoop strapped to his pack and takes every opportunity to get other hikers to hula. Photo by Michael Kodas, The Hartford Courant

HANOVER, NEW HAMPSHIRE

The wilderness is segregated, but not because of any spoken rules. Dan (Wing-foot) Bruce, trail guru and author of the annually updated *The Thru-hiker's Handbook*, says the fastest-growing segment of hiker population is women, but by far most

Ward Cridland of Lake Charles, Louisiana, rides his mountain bike off the Stratton Mountain gondola. Riders at Stratton can use the gondola to get to the top of the mountain and then take a wild ride down one of the mountain's ski trails. A round-trip ride on the gondola is free for through-hikers. Photo by Michael Kodas, The Hartford Courant

Lalena Storms and her daughter Amber, 4, enjoy the water that rushes through Clarendon Gorge in Clarendon, Vermont. Lalena was born in Vermont, and the family has just returned to the state "to stay." The family spent the day visiting places that were special to Lalena during her youth. She said the last time she visited the gorge was after her father died. Photo by Michael Kodas, The Hartford Courant

Sunrise over the Green Mountains of Vermont can be seen from the summit of Stratton Mountain, birthplace of the Appalachian Trail.
Photo by Michael Kodas, The Hartford Courant

Appalachian Trail hikers are men.

We were just leaving The Inn at Long Trail at Sherburne Pass, Vermont, for our third week of hiking when Maine Rose shooed away the other hikers—all men—and leaned toward me conspiratorially.

"This is woman talk," she said. "When you look at me, do you see a fat woman?"

I didn't. I saw Beverly Hugo (Maine Rose), 48, of Portland, Maine, a short woman of solid build with well-defined quadriceps that I'd only a moment ago been surreptitiously admiring. She started the trail in March at Springer Mountain in Georgia weighing 210 pounds. She's carried her backpack for nearly 1,700 miles and dropped 43 pounds. A single mother, she has built a house, started several businesses, lived abroad and—so she could hike—arranged six months of child care for her 15-year-old daughter and 12-year-old son. But Rose still worries that she's fat. I'll just bet not too many men out here are worrying about that.

Most girls have fenced off their wilder selves by puberty. We may start out mouthy, loud, happy and brave, but then we leave the wilderness and shrink ourselves to fit the station wagon or office desk, because that is where we think we are supposed to be.

The civilized world is far more scary, but we move all the monsters outdoors. When I told friends I was going to hike the trail for a month, they asked, "Yeah, but are you taking a gun?" It got sillier. In March, I attended a talk in Tolland, Connecticut, by a local woman who through-hiked in 1992. Offstage, in private, she suggested I wear panty liners. Ha, thought I. That would imply I'm going to wear panties.

Of course women care about hygiene— they ask Dan Bruce questions about that as well as about safety—but they are more concerned about eating properly and carrying that pack. Still, the slightly different interests

Joe Fennelly (Cool Breeze), a two-time through-hiker from Cheshire, Connecticut, has a laugh while putting steps and a water bar into the Appalachian Trail near River Road in Sherburne, Vermont. Fennelly works for the Green Mountain Club volunteer trail crew. Photo by Michael Kodas, The Hartford Courant

Beverly Hugo (Maine Rose) pauses along the Appalachian Trail/Long Trail near Sherburne, Vermont. Photo by Michael Kodas, The Hartford Courant

of hiking women and men is a dicey subject that even the egalitarian Bruce hasn't solved. He has been promising a trail book for women, but the deadline keeps getting bumped as he tries to write informatively and inoffensively.

"It's a very tricky book to write," Bruce said. "We want to give practical information. I think generally women are cautious in American life, and rightly so. When I say cautious, I mean they have to be aware that they might be perceived as being vulnerable."

"Are you hiking alone?" an old man asked me in a white birch stand near Gifford Woods State Park in Vermont. I didn't want to scare him. I told him I was hiking in a group—and I was, if you count all the other hikers.

"That's good," he said. "You read of such awful things," like rapes and murders on the trail, so much so that a 1992 Appalachian Bulletin advised women not to hike alone. In her book, *A Woman's Journey*, Cindy Ross, an art student who "got tired of looking down 18 stories to diseased oaks, diseased pigeons and confused humans running the maze," wrote: "Alone I take life much more seriously." She started the trail unsure of her ability to hike, but by the time she reached October Mountain in Vermont, figured: "Oh hell, I'm doing the rest of it."

Maine Rose's early trail conditioning is something to be remembered. Bruce says: "There really is no reason why a woman in decent physical health and condition—not even great condition but just decent—can't hike the Appalachian Trail for whatever period, be it a day hike or 2,000 miles."

Male or female, the trail boils you down to your essence. If you are brave off trail, you are brave on. Still, after talking to Rose, I hiked two days ahead of Michael. It was 21 miles over trail relocations that included countless puds—pointless ups and downs. I have come to expect to be rewarded with a view when I climb a hill, and there were none to be had for two solid days. On the second night, he caught me at the Wintturi shelter, a well-maintained, three-sided cabin near a spring. I pitched my tent 20 feet away, and just as we all settled in, coyotes began calling each other from the ridges surrounding us. I felt as if I'd fallen into a spooky movie. I know coyotes avoid contact with humans, but I opened my knife and left it where I

Maine Rose reads her mail in the backyard of the Panarchy fraternity house at Dartmouth University in Hanover, New Hampshire. The fraternity is one of several at the university that put up hikers for a small fee or chores done around the house. Photo by Michael Kodas, The Hartford Courant

Chris Warren (Grim Creeper), of Union, Kentucky, known on the trail for her high mileage, walks the trail over Kinsman Mountain in the White Mountains of New Hampshire. Grim Creeper through-hiked the trail in less than five months in 1993 and wanted to beat that time this year. In June she got off the trail in Cheshire, Massachusetts, intending to give up her hike. Two months later she decided to come back and allowed herself a month to hike from Cheshire, Massachusetts, to the trail's finish. She hikes an average of 24 miles a day. Photo by Michael Kodas, The Hartford Courant

Michael Kodas warms his hands while getting some protection from winds approaching 70 mph on the summit of Mount Moosilauke, the first mountain the Appalachian Adventure team has crossed in the White Mountains of New Hampshire. Kodas's hands were numbed by the high winds and 40° temperatures on the summit of the foreboding mountain. Photo by Susan Campbell, The Hartford Courant

Silver Hill is one of a few campsites with a well. Pump three times for icy water. Illustration by Phil Lohman.

could grab it—and dozed off quickly. Fortunately, in all my thrashing around that night, I did not land on that blade.

With some 27 miles left to get to Hanover, New Hampshire, Michael and I promised each other we'd cover big ground. We got up early and took off on one of the more scenic hikes I've had so far. I climbed a hill and I got a view—twice—of the distant White Mountains, where the last ridge was only a slightly darker blue than the sky. Coming out of the forest, I saw a picture-perfect farm, all in postcard weather. In one pasture, I passed through chin-high grass and remembered the Daisy BB gun I carried as a girl. I once raised it and put a BB through the heart of a barn swallow who'd surprised me at my grandparents' farm. It fell in a puff of dust at my feet and I ran crying to the house. I was lost in the reverie when I surprised nine wild turkeys. They arose with a shout (mine) and just cleared the hickory trees that separated two fields.

Later that day, I lingered too long over chocolate milk, chips, dip and a Mars bar at the village store in West Hartford, Vermont. Michael looked at the sky and said matter-of-factly that we'd have to night-hike some of the last 4 miles to Happy Hill Cabin. I felt a brief moment of panic. Night-hiking is a curve ball I hadn't intended to pitch to myself. I took off at a fast clip, thinking maybe the dark wouldn't overtake me. That was the phrase I used to scare myself: "overtake."

But the first section was a long ascent through a spruce forest, and by the time I'd gone 2 miles, I was thinking of Maine Rose behind me. She won't night-hike. She pitches her tent by the side of the trail if she has to. I wanted to make the shelter, so I pressed on.

The woods get dark first, and before long all I could make out were the white blazes painted on trees every 30 feet or so. I didn't so much see the trail as feel it. I stepped over spruce roots and rocks and went around curves I sensed were there. I came to a clearing nearly a mile from the cabin and surprised a doe feeding on the tall grass there. She headed straight up the trail. I reentered the pitch-black woods, half expecting to see her waiting for me.

Finally, still a quarter of a mile from the cabin, I put on my headlamp and followed the white blazes to the oldest (and most rundown) cabin on the trail. I made my bed on a door propped on the porch rails, so that my feet and my head stuck out from underneath the roof. There were so many stars that I could hardly see the night sky. A bat fluttered by, and when a coyote howled from a nearby hill, I drifted off to sleep, only a little scared. I was the girl who used to live here.

FRANCONIA NOTCH, NEW HAMPSHIRE

On to the rugged White Mountains, where above timberline there dwell hardy plants that survive unprotected in the summit's unearthly weather but take 20 years to regenerate from a wayward bootstep.

Susan Campbell yawns as she awakens in a cement pipe in a hikers' parking lot in Kinsman Notch, New Hampshire. Campbell and Michael Kodas spent the night in the pipes after hiking over Mount Moosilauke in New Hampshire's White Mountains. Photo by Michael Kodas, The Hartford Courant

To the Whites, so named by early European sailors, who spotted the snow on the summits from the sea during the summer.

To the Whites, where on this, the end of Michael's and my respective eight- and four-week hiking adventures, I am sure I will get my butt kicked.

All along, I have heard that the White Mountains are the behemoths of the trail. Clingman's Dome is taller, but the Whites are relentless. Northbound hikers are told that entry into New Hampshire marks 80 percent of their distance, and 50 percent of their work.

I am a nonhiker. For months, I woke up with visions of myself shivering by the side of a mountain trail, quietly dying. Even three weeks on the trail have not convinced me that I can do this.

Maybe fear colored my mood early on. On our first full day out of Hanover, we hiked an uneventful 15 miles, followed by another nearly that long to the Hexacuba shelter.

Boston artist Patricia Burson paints one of the cascades of the Beaver Brook, which runs beside the Beaver Brook Trail, a section of the Appalachian Trail that descends from Mount Moosilauke into Kinsman Notch, New Hampshire. The trail is so steep here that wooden steps and metal guardrails have been installed on it to make it passable, but the waterfalls make the effort worth it.
Photo by Michael Kodas, The Hartford Courant

Coming up was Mount Moosilauke, my first taste of above-timberline hiking, where the land feels the full force of violent storms that can blow up in a heartbeat. I hadn't so much hiked as stomped. I was tired of the food, tired of waking up cold at night, tired of missing my family.

That night in my tent, I lay in my bag liner—far too thin coverage for the chilly late summer nights. In the tent next door, Cory Rearis of North Lauderdale, Florida, started talking about the stars—something he doesn't see in heavily lit Florida.

"I want to see some wild animals," he said. "Have you seen any wild animals yet?"

As he lay there talking in the dark, a 19-year-old man with a boy's wonder, my mood lifted. Maybe this is what the woods are all about—finding that child wonder that escapes with a loud whoop as you top a summit and see honest-to-God purple mountains' majesty.

And besides, up ahead were still those otherworldly plants, the subalpine of black spruce and balsam firs. Walking through them is like walking through Christmas.

And about 1,500 feet higher dwells krummholz, dwarfed trees that look like unhealthy lawn shrubs. I had only read of them, and wanted to see them for myself. But my real interest was the alpine plants—Diapensia and mountain heath—that grow above timberline. Something about a tough dwarf willow that can survive anything but human touch appeals to me.

The day we climbed Moosilauke, a mist settled into the trees like watery cobwebs. We hiked steadily, and as we neared the top we sang Warren Zevon, our answer to camp tunes.

Nearer the summit, though, the singing ceased. The winds, which we estimated were gusting at 70 mph, made walking difficult and talking—unless you screamed in some-

Franconia Notch, New Hampshire, with Cannon Mountain on the left and the Franconia Ridge on the right. Photo by Michael Kodas, The Hartford Courant

one's ear—impossible. The mist that was so pretty down below was now being driven into our faces like sand, and the straps and strings from the rain gear we'd donned whipped around like angry snakes.

It would have been smart to leave the summit quickly, but we were intrigued by the wind, the noise and the moonscape before us. We were only able to see from cairn to cairn as we climbed. When we reached the ruins of an old hotel on the summit, Michael snapped pictures as I tried to step over the rocks, but after 20 minutes he said, "We need to think about hypothermia." He didn't have to say it twice.

He loaded his cameras, and we made what felt like a drunken dash for the quarter mile from the summit to the treeline, shouting but not hearing a thing. I ran ahead and turned twice to see Michael walk-running, head down, behind me. When we reached the treeline, out of breath and laughing, we shouted and gave each other high fives. It was dangerous, scary and grand, grand fun, and the mile-long cascade along Beaver Brook trail was a perfect end to the day. The rocky and

steep trail took my entire attention, but I stopped frequently just to look at the patterns that had been cut into the rock by the falling water. The notch was named for Asa Kinsman, a pioneer who in the 1780s took a wrong turn at Plymouth and, rather than admit his mistake and turn his oxen back, hacked his way through the wilderness to set up his homestead.

The next day, joined by *Courant* graphics artist Phil Lohman, Michael and I climbed hand over hand over rock tumbles to the twin peaks of South and North Kinsman. We were walking with Chris Warren (Grim Creeper), of Union, Kentucky, who had returned to the trail after leaving it for two months to attend to family affairs such as weddings. Grim and I reached the summit first and looked out over a rumpled purple-and-blue blanket of the Whites.

"Oh, look," she said, pointing behind me. The sun had broken through the clouds and given a layer of pink sunset to the purple landscape. I began yelling and only stopped when I ran out of things to say.

Mount Katahdin, the northern terminus of the Appalachian Trail, as seen from the West Branch of the Penobscot River in Maine. Photo by John Patriquin, Maine Sunday Telegram

NORTH TO THE WILDERNESS

A U G U S T   2 4 – O C T O B E R   1 ,   1 9 9 5

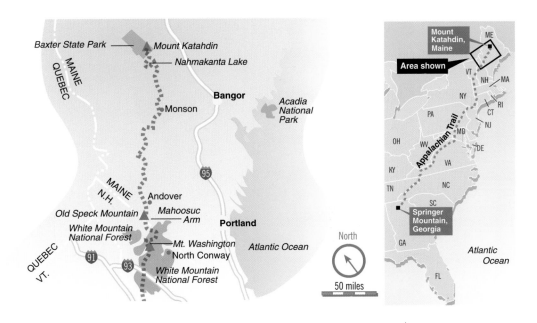

PINKHAM NOTCH,
NEW HAMPSHIRE

**Text by
Lloyd Ferriss**

**Photography by
John Ewing**

Fifty-mph winds and 40° temperatures slowed our hike over the high Franconia Range. By late afternoon, the August sun was sinking, and our campsite was still 3 miles ahead in the 723,296-acre White Mountain National Forest. That's where we met Moses.

It wasn't hard to see how Robert Nose came by his trail name. He is 66, with a gray beard, gray hair and intense brown eyes.

Unlike us, Moses wasn't worried about reaching camp by dark. "As I walk along," said the resident of the U.S. Virgin Islands, "I ask the Lord for a place to

Bob Nose (Moses) takes a break near Mount Lafayette. A section hiker, Nose spends winters chartering his 32-foot cutter in the Virgin Islands.
Photo by John Ewing, Maine Sunday Telegram

Dave Gilligen, an Appalachian Mountain Club hut crew member, makes dough for the day's bread at the Galehead Hut in the Pemigewasset Wilderness area of the White Mountains National Forest in New Hampshire. AMC huts provide food and shelter for the many hikers who use the state's trail system. Photo by John Ewing, Maine Sunday Telegram

sleep. And I always find the most wonderful, soft places."

Maybe Moses was onto something. Photographer John Ewing and I reached the Garfield Ridge campsite with daylight to spare. We set up our tents on dry ground and, moments after driving in the last tent stake, rain came in torrents.

In the days afterward, we made our way over ridge lines and valleys of the lush green Pemigewasset Wilderness, a name taken from an Abenaki word meaning swift current. It perfectly describes the Pemigewasset River and other sparkling streams that course through these mountains.

And it is wilderness. In more than 50 miles of trail that take hikers from Franconia Notch, New Hampshire, to the Pemigewasset and up and over the magnificent Presidential Range, the area is cut by just one major highway. Clear nights reveal brilliant stars and planets. There is no light pollution.

But the White Mountain National Forest is a crowded place, too. It has four major ski

Signposts mark the trail in New Hampshire's White Mountain National Forest. Photo by John Ewing, Maine Sunday Telegram

areas and 1,000 miles of hiking trails. Hunters and fishermen use it, as do timber companies harvesting pulp for paper and birch wood for furniture.

It is so popular, in fact, that in 1994 the National Park Service put the White Mountain National Forest in its "urban forest" category, along with 14 other heavily used playgrounds, such as the Angeles National Forest in California.

To protect this fragile ecosystem, environmentalists have crafted regulations that, among other things, restrict group camping, camping near trails and camping above the timberline. If there is a downside to such efforts, it is a loss of what some have called the freedom of the hills.

In Franconia, 10 young hikers from the University of New Hampshire's Outing Club had just received a $150 citation for group hiking without a permit when we met them. They were headed to Mount Washington when a ranger stopped and ticketed them.

Kara Loiko, a leader of the club's trip and a student of environmental conservation at the university, seemed perplexed. "At first I

Emily and Tom McCall, day hikers from Rochester, New York, enjoy lunch and a scenic vista from the vicinity of Mount Lafayette. Photo by John Ewing, Maine Sunday Telegram

TOP: *The Mount Washington Cog Railway ferries passengers to the summit of Mount Washington in New Hampshire. Hikers often find crowds of tourists atop the mountain, which is home to some of the harshest weather in the world.* Photo by John Ewing, Maine Sunday Telegram

BOTTOM: *Lloyd Ferriss (Tattoo) hikes along a ridge toward New Hampshire's Mount Lafayette. The stone cairn marks the trail.* Photo by John Ewing, Maine Sunday Telegram

Mount Washington's wild weather

Experienced AT hikers approach New Hampshire's Mount Washington with caution. The mountain—at 6,288 feet the highest in the Northeast and the third highest on the trail—is notorious for deadly, winterlike storms even in summer. Winds at the summit reach hurricane force (73 mph) an average of 104 days a year. On August 24, for example, the wind hit 94 mph and by the next morning the temperature had fallen to 32°. Here's why the weather on Mount Washington can be so bad.

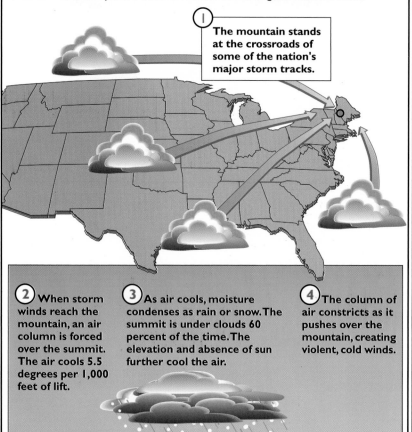

① The mountain stands at the crossroads of some of the nation's major storm tracks.

② When storm winds reach the mountain, an air column is forced over the summit. The air cools 5.5 degrees per 1,000 feet of lift.

③ As air cools, moisture condenses as rain or snow. The summit is under clouds 60 percent of the time. The elevation and absence of sun further cool the air.

④ The column of air constricts as it pushes over the mountain, creating violent, cold winds.

WIND

Mount Washington records

	SEPTEMBER	OVERALL
Record-high temp.	67° (1960)	72° (Aug. 1975)
Record-low temp.	9° (1992)	– 47° (Jan. 1934)
Max. precip.	14.07 in. (1938)	25.56 in. (Feb. 1969)
Max. precip. in 24 hours	5.38 in. (1985)	10.38 in. (Feb. 1970)
Max. snow, ice, hail	7.8 in. (1949)	172.8 in. (Feb. 1969)
Max. snow, ice, hail in 24 hours	7.7 in. (1986)	49.3 in. (Feb. 1969)*
Peak gust	174 mph (1979)	231 mph (April 1934)*

*World record

PAUL KOLSTI / Maine Sunday Telegram

thought he was joking," she said. "I've never gotten a ticket for parking. Now I have a ticket for hiking."

Severe as such measures may seem, their intent is noble: to protect some of the most spectacular yet fragile scenery in the United States from being trampled by its admirers. Near Lakes of the Clouds, I stopped to stare at a small, federally restricted area that is off-limits to hikers, home of a little yellow alpine flower called Robbins dwarf cinquefoil. Globally endangered, it grows there and nowhere else on earth.

Ironically, this forest, home to such delicacy, is the site of some of the most brutal weather anywhere. On April 12, 1934, Mount Washington endured a singular event in climatological history: a wind gust of 231 mph. Nowhere on the surface of the earth has that measurement been equaled.

Toward noon of that morning, the crew at the small summit weather observatory knew they were in for something special. Gusts of 200 mph raked the summit. Alexander A. McKenzie, the only meteorologist on staff that day who is still living, recalls seeing a window bend inward, then pop back to normal.

At about 1 P.M., McKenzie clocked gusts of 229 mph. There was a lull. At 1:21 P.M., the building—chained to the rock summit— shook violently. The anemometer read 231 mph. "Will anyone believe us?" McKenzie recalls thinking.

Hikers take in the view atop a rock outcropping in Maine's Mahoosuc Mountains. Photo by John Ewing, Maine Sunday Telegram

Today, the accuracy of the recording is unquestioned. Yet there has never been a repeat performance.

Mount Washington is scoured by violent weather because it is square in the path of three storm tracks—from the west, north and south. According to Peter Crane, the associate director of programs at the Mount Washington Observatory Resource Center in North Conway, New Hampshire, the wind reaches 120 mph every few years.

But why has the 1934 record never been matched? McKenzie thinks he knows. Back then, the observatory—which has since been replaced—stood on the eastern edge of the summit and had, McKenzie said, "an unobstructed view as far as the wind is concerned." The present building is more protected, and may be buffeted less as a result, he said.

McKenzie, retired now and living in Eaton, New Hampshire, calls the observa-

TOP: *Lloyd Ferriss makes his way over boulders in Maine's Mahoosuc Notch, reportedly the most difficult mile on the trail. Photo by John Ewing, Maine Sunday Telegram*

BOTTOM: *Through-hiker Brian Vargo (Early Riser) from Muncy, Pennsylvania, watches as Jill Laramie (Chameleon) from Rutland, Vermont, makes her way up and out of a hole in the boulders of the Mahoosuc Notch in Maine. Photo by John Ewing, Maine Sunday Telegram*

tory every evening. He wants to know about the wind. Always the wind. "The observers look forward to that contact," said Crane. "It's a connection—a connection with a tradition."

ANDOVER, MAINE

I squeezed under the first of the house-size boulders like a tortoise with a 40-pound shell. Safely through, I clambered to the top of the next giant and leaped to still another. Then it was back to the dirt for more crawling.

So it went for the next hour as we jumped, shimmied and otherwise scrambled through Mahoosuc Notch, a steep valley filled with massive boulders that is thought to be the toughest mile of the trail.

The boulders are jammed next to and atop one another, a jungle of huge blocks. The valley is so shaded by rock that patches of last year's crusty snow survive into September. Here the trail, as though planned by a congress of devils, forces hikers to slither like snakes.

Struggling with us was Rebecca Clark (Otter Raven Maniac), a 24-year-old through-hiker from Windham, Maine. "Exhilarating," she called Mahoosuc Notch. Tough going, I called it.

You get no breaks around here. Just south of the notch are steep peaks separated by deep valleys. North is rugged Mahoosuc Arm Mountain, followed by 4,180-foot Old Speck Mountain. This is no mere walk in the woods.

I am beaten up and humbled by these mountains. My knees ache. I crawl into my tent at sunset and sleep effortlessly until sunrise. The sleep brings recovery, followed by another beating.

Yet the trail is nothing less than awesome as it winds through western Maine. "They told me how tough Mahoosuc Notch was, but they didn't tell me how beautiful it is," said David Gates (Peace Dog), from Hudson Falls, New York. "It sure isn't Kansas."

In early September it is turning colder in the northern Appalachians. Leaves on poplars and birches are yellow. Though John and I sweat in the valleys, the wind has a nip on the summits. We scurry to our packs for warm clothing.

David Gates (Peace Dog) of Hudson Falls, New York, maneuvers over boulders in Mahoosuc Notch. Photo by John Ewing, Maine Sunday Telegram

"Hardening" the trail

As more people hike it, the AT has come under stress from overuse and erosion. Each year, 350 to 400 volunteers from the Maine Appalachian Trail Club work to make the trail more passable yet "harden" it against human impact at the same time. Here are some of their trail-hardening techniques.

Split-log bridge ▶

Provides dry, stable walkway over wet areas. In Maine, maintainers have built thousands of feet of these bridges over natural bogs and old logging roads.

Water bar ▲

This key antierosion tool intercepts water as it runs down the trail and directs it elsewhere.

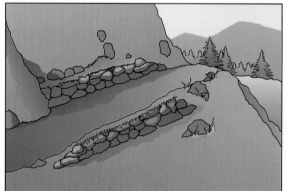

Cribbing and sidehilling ▲

Rock cribbing shores up hillsides and stabilizes trail edges. Sidehilling prevents erosion by angling the trail across the downward flow of water.

Rock steps ▲

Valuable for preventing water erosion, especially in steep areas with thin topsoils.

PETE GORSKI / Maine Sunday Telegram

After a hot day of hiking in Maine's Mahoosuc Mountains, Lloyd Ferriss couldn't wait for a refreshing dip in Speck Pond. Photo by John Ewing, Maine Sunday Telegram

Richard Churchill, a botanist from South Portland, Maine, walked with us. He explained how alpine plants adapt to this changing season and to the mountain winter that follows.

Churchill showed us how diapensia, a small mountaintop plant, extends its growing season by creating its own environment. As its rubbery leaves change from green to rusty red, the red absorbs more heat. The plant's temperature goes up three or four degrees, and it continues to grow despite a general cooling of the weather.

Fir trees adapt, too. While their needles grow relatively flat on the branch in the lowlands, on mountaintops they surround the branch like tight-fitting porcupine quills. The cluster, said Churchill, keeps the tree from drying out in extreme conditions.

Despite Churchill's wonderful diversions, the Mahoosucs strained muscles and mind. Still, there was occasional relief for the weary body.

Beyond Mahoosuc Notch, I followed the

Paul P. Johnson, Jr., a retired forest ranger from Monmouth, Maine, clears borders of the trail near Stratton, Maine. Johnson maintains 4.6 miles of trail that he's "adopted" between Sabbath Day Pond and the Little Swift River Pond campsite. He's one of more than 4,000 volunteers who keep the trail in good shape. Photo by John Ewing, Maine Sunday Telegram

example of Jessica Clymer (Flower) of Ohio and dived into Speck Pond. It is glacier-created and, at 3,500 feet, is the highest pond in Maine. It's also colder than the North Atlantic. It was a short dip.

Later I hiked out of Grafton Notch. To my left, low-afternoon sunlight glowed through yellow and green birch leaves. The woods were still and silent.

At that moment, I wished the trail would go on forever.

STRATTON, MAINE

The trail sloped gently down a wooded hillside above Little Swift River Pond, and we could see Paul P. Johnson, Jr., below us: a small figure in shirtsleeves, bent over a clump of yard-high balsam fir. Johnson's shears made a rhythmic sound as he pruned the trees back from the trail.

A retired forest ranger from Monmouth, Maine, Johnson straightened and smiled. We noticed the big circled arrow symbol on his white shirt, and the words "Maine Appalachian Trail Club Volunteer."

Johnson is 59, with curly hair and friendly brown eyes. In a way, his is the face of the trail. Three to six times each year, he grooms 4.6 miles of trail that he has adopted between Sabbath Day Pond and the Little Swift River Pond campsite. One year he cleared 160 trees that had been knocked onto his section by a storm.

Up and down this incredibly long trail, from Springer Mountain to Katahdin, hun-dreds of volunteers in 32 trail clubs labor as Johnson does. They build water bars and lean-tos and they clean privies—all to help others enjoy the trail. "We do it," Johnson told me, "because we take pride in being part of something so much bigger than we are."

As I watched Johnson selectively lop trees and brush from the trailside, I felt as if I could see a living history of the trail. It was 58 years ago that volunteers and members of the Civilian Conservation Corps cleared the final link of the trail on a ridge near Sugar-

Lloyd Ferriss takes a lunch break of peanut-butter sandwiches on the trail near Rangeley, Maine. Photo by John Ewing, Maine Sunday Telegram

Annie Law, of Honeybrook, Pennsylvania, is all smiles as she takes a break along the trail near Andover, Maine. She began hiking sections of the trail in 1978 and is on her last section. Hiking with her is her friend, Anne Foster, of Newark, Delaware.

September moves toward October. Fallen birch leaves litter the ground like drops of gold. In the black trail soil, the deep hoofprints of moose mingle with shallower prints left by hikers. It's clear that summer is dying.

A day after seeing Johnson, as I climbed Saddleback Mountain, the temperature dropped to about 35° and I was buffeted by high winds and rain. Nighttime temperatures are now low enough for some hikers to sleep with wool caps on their heads.

"A few weeks ago we had heatstroke to worry about. Now it's hypothermia," said Rob Adamson (Rob of Loxley).

With Katahdin just 200 miles away, the trail in September belongs to through-hikers. It's narrow—often no more than 18 inches wide—and the weekend hiker has almost disappeared. On one cloudless, late summer day, as I climbed the twin summits of Crocker Mountain, I found myself alone except for my thoughts.

That was the Appalachian Trail as it used to be. There was Benton MacKaye's dream, an uncrowded footpath through the wilderness.

I thought of the lean-tos in which I'd slept in recent weeks, shelters with hikers jammed so close that you couldn't see the floorboards. I thought about the Lakes of the Clouds hut, where 90 overnight hikers brushed elbows at dinner tables.

About 2,000 through-hikers have departed Springer Mountain annually in recent years. It's closer to 3,000 this year. What happens

loaf Mountain. Myles Fenton, who toiled with the CCC, told me about those glory days before I started my hike. "My tour in the CCC was a feast, and the Appalachian Trail was dessert," Fenton said.

It's that spirit that keeps the much-used trail in good condition, said Brian King of the Appalachian Trail Conference in Harpers Ferry, West Virginia. In 1994, said King, 4,538 men and women worked the trail without pay. "A lot of hikers think the trail just exists," King said. "They think the government takes care of it, but it doesn't. That would cost $4 million a year—just for the time volunteers put in."

Ironically, few through-hikers end up maintaining the trail the way Johnson does. "Through-hikers are often at a transition point in life," said King. "They're just out of school, or in a mid-career change. They have the next part of their transition to do."

Transition is everywhere on the trail as

A white blaze and the Appalachian Trail symbol mark the crossing of the trail and Route 17 near Oquossuc, Maine. Mooselookmeguntic Lake is in the distance. Photo by John Ewing, Maine Sunday Telegram

when the number climbs to 6,000? Or 12,000?

Benjamin Harth, a hiker I had met days before, shared my concern for the trail. He's 24 and a recent graduate of a college in central Florida, where he studied philosophy.

"I think everyone should have a chance to hike the trail," he told me, "but there are just too many people. The trail is in danger of being loved to death."

I thought of Harth's warning, and I knew he was right. But by some miracle, I was alone for once, and I was able to enjoy the trail as a wilderness path: step by step, rock by rock, adventure by adventure.

MONSON, MAINE

Text by Edie Lau

By the time Trooper and his companions reached Pierce Pond, they were rowdy with joy. They had just completed 2,000 miles—one in a string of milestones they would pass, boom, boom, boom, in the next few days.

"You hit Maine, and you're like, wow, it's the last state," said Trooper, a 26-year-old from Milford, New Hampshire, whose real

Edie Lau and her sister Wendy Lau approach the summit of West Peak on Bigelow Mountain, near Stratton, Maine. The Bigelow Preserve, created in 1976, is a popular camping spot. Photo by John Ewing, Maine Sunday Telegram

Edie Lau splashes cool water on her face at Flagstaff Lake in the Bigelow Range. Photo by John Ewing, Maine Sunday Telegram

name is Michael Dennis. "There are so many milestones from here: the 2,000-mile mark, the Kennebec River, and then Monson—the last town."

These brisk days are filled with lasts for the northbound tribe of through-hikers.

It was 29° and clear as the three of us—John Ewing, my sister, Wendy Lau, and me—stepped into the Bigelow Preserve. The mountains were beginning to blush with fall colors. Near the gigantic ponds in the valleys, we shushed one another to better hear the warble of the loons.

Even to those who've spent six months trekking America's eastern woods, the trail in west-central Maine is impressive for its variety. There are maples and birches, evergreens and ferns, mushrooms and mosses, dales and bogs.

"Maine is really different," said John P. Smith of Columbus, Ohio, a hiker with legs that stretch forever and the catchy trail name Forest Gimp. "Maine is more rugged than any other state. It has more ponds, and more kinds of wildlife."

Through-hikers take a break to try their hand at climbing a rock wall near the trail in Andover, Maine. Photo by John Ewing, Maine Sunday Telegram

Forest Gimp was one of four spirited hikers whose 2,000-mile celebration at the edge of Pierce Pond we witnessed. It was a fitting place for happy people, a fish-filled pool that tumbled over rocks and formed waterfalls worthy of a Japanese tea garden, then rushed toward the Kennebec River 3 miles beyond.

The Kennebec is the most hazardous water crossing of the trail. Its chief danger stems from two dams upstream, which may release walls of water without warning.

Ten years ago, a 61-year-old woman from Georgia drowned trying to ford the Kennebec. Since then, trail overseers have provided a free ferry. It's the only ferry on the footpath; officially, it's the right way to get across.

But Steve Longley, the ferryman for nine years, knows that hikers are an independent lot. So he lays out their options: cross in his canoe; ford the river while he carries the backpack by canoe and stands by watchfully; swim across, again with him ferrying the pack and standing by; or go it alone and hold only themselves accountable.

Trooper chose to swim. Untold frigid strokes later, he stood on the opposite bank, triumphant but humbled by the effort. "I feel alive!" he declared. "Nothing can stop us now."

We wouldn't see that much water again for some time.

As we left the Kennebec a light rain fell, a rare occurrence this summer in the parched Maine forest. A drought has reduced springs

and brooks to damp spots, forcing hikers to carry more water than usual. That weighs heavily on them—literally, since each quart adds two pounds.

"Whenever you meet people passing, one of the first questions you ask is, 'How's the water up ahead?'" said Leonard Adkins of Roanoke, Virginia. He and his wife, Laurie, have hiked the world over, usually drawing water from springs; on this trip, for the first time, they used iodine to purify pond water.

The drought drove us to Monson ahead of schedule. We had nearly run out of water.

Downed trees form a bridge across a bog in Maine. Photo by John Ewing, Maine Sunday Telegram

There isn't a lot to Monson, which coalesced a century ago around a slate factory. Its landmarks now include a convenience store, a restaurant, a furniture factory and Shaw's Boarding House—a trail institution created by sheer chance.

The trail winds its way through a section of Maine forest near Monson. Photo by John Ewing, Maine Sunday Telegram

Keith and Pat Shaw used to run a boarding home for mentally ill and retarded people. One June day in 1977, a hiker asked the Shaws if he could stay the night. They said yes.

The next day, that hiker told a man headed south about Shaw's. The word spread, and that summer, the Shaws traded their board-and-care license for a lodging-and-meals ticket. Now in their 19th season, the Shaws have fed and bedded between 18,000 and 19,000 hikers.

A bed at Shaw's costs between $12 and $20, depending on the room. The all-you-can-eat breakfast is $4.50, dinner $8. But when Larry and Marilyn Plott arrived with only $2, they weren't turned away. Instead, the Idaho couple, who call themselves The Spuds, were allowed to pay their way by doing chores. The place was so friendly that The Spuds considered staying an extra day, even after more money arrived. After all, there would be no such hospitality in the next section of trail, the 100-mile wilderness.

Water tumbles over rocks en route to the Kennebec River at Pierce Pond. Photo by John Ewing, Maine Sunday Telegram

Steve Longley works for the Maine Appalachian Trail Club, ferrying hikers across the Kennebec River in Maine. The river is considered the trail's most dangerous water crossing, because upstream dams can release water at any moment. Photo by John Ewing, Maine Sunday Telegram

NAHMAKANTA LAKE, MAINE

She stopped and looked at us balefully, then resumed chewing. The cow moose was not about to let a couple of silly hikers with cameras for faces interrupt her lunch.

We were skirting a bog called Mud Pond when we saw the beast. Her hide, the color of dark chocolate, looked so velvety soft in the sun that I wished I could pet her.

People had assured me that I'd see moose in Maine's north country, but this was sooner than I had expected. We were only 5 miles into the region commonly called the 100-mile wilderness.

The so-called wilderness is the final stretch for through-hikers. It's a land of paradoxes, physically and spiritually. Tired bodies rejoice at the thought of ending the 2,158-mile journey. But hearts hesitate, unwilling to trade the peace of the forest for the stress of the outside world.

In a way, the 100-mile wilderness reflects the through-hiker's divided mind. It is a place where hikers are as apt to hear the growl of a chainsaw as the crash of a moose. It's a land of gurgling springs, roaring waterfalls and loon song that is accessible not only to backpackers but to day hikers via logging roads, boats and float planes.

En route to Monson, Maine, Edie Lau and sister Wendy cross the Piscataquis River in Maine by means of a beaver dam. Photo by John Ewing, Maine Sunday Telegram

Through-hikers chat outside the Caratunk General Store in Maine. Towns and stores are popular stops for hikers looking to resupply, eat junk food or use telephones. Photo by John Ewing, Maine Sunday Telegram

You don't necessarily know that when you enter the wilderness near Monson. A sign warns hikers to carry 10 days' worth of food.

Amy Zegelbone, a 25-year-old through-hiker from Black Mountain, North Carolina, was relieved to reach remote northern Maine; she had found the White Mountains of New Hampshire unpleasantly crowded. "I thought, 'finally!'" said Zegelbone, who goes by the trail name Night Sprite. So she was taken aback when she encountered day hikers who had entered from a gravel road.

She tried to contain her disappointment. "A lot of through-hikers think, 'Oh, this is my trail,'" she said. "I think everyone should enjoy it." Others are less charitable; notebooks at trail lean-tos are filled with complaints.

"What wilderness?! I can hear the lumber trucks right now!" wrote "The Grateful Greenpeace Guy" in the Long Pond Stream lean-to register.

In fact, trail overseers don't call this a wilderness. To them, the 99.4 miles of woods uninterrupted by paved roads is simply "Monson to Abol Bridge."

"There's no special name for it," David Field, chairman of the Appalachian Trail Conference, said in an interview before I started my hike. Field, a forestry professor at the University of Maine, said the problem with the term *wilderness* is that hikers con-

fuse it with government-designated wildernesses, in which activities such as logging are not allowed.

The 100-mile wilderness, Field said, "is a working forest. Has been for 400 years."

Still, he said, "It's wild. It's primitive. To probably 90 percent of users, it's as wild as they want. It's wilderness with a lowercase *w*."

Two mountain ranges jut from this otherwise flat terrain. I spent one leisurely lunchtime on Barren Ledges, a rock overlook

Edie Lau bundles up against the cold as she eats a meal in the 100-mile wilderness. Photo by John Ewing, Maine Sunday Telegram

on the Barren Chairback Range. It was surprisingly warm for mid-September, nearly 80° in the sun. Ravens flew overhead in lazy circles.

Relishing the day with me was my hiking companion, Joyce Mailman, a 37-year-old backpacking fanatic from Saco, Maine. Mailman and I watched moving dark spots on Lake Onawa far below and fancied they were moose swimming. We stared quietly at the brooding hump of Boarstone Mountain rising behind the lake. Way out on the horizon, we could make out the Bigelow Range, a jagged blue shadow at the edge of the sky.

Wildlife is abundant. Some 30,000 moose live in Maine, and chances are good that hik-

Alex Kopista cooks up a "feed-a-thon" at Antlers Camp on the shore of Lower Jo-Mary Lake. He and Cat Eich, both former through-hikers, like to pop up unexpectedly with food for ravenous hikers. Photo by John Ewing, Maine Sunday Telegram

ers here will glimpse one. Loons are far less numerous—the Maine Audubon Society estimates 4,000 breeding pairs in the state—but their presence is far greater because of their distinctive songs.

Bedded down in a lean-to one night, I

defied the near-freezing cold and poked my face out of my sleeping bag so I could better hear the loons from nearby Pemadumcook Lake. In the dark, their calls are ghostly. Perhaps that's appropriate, because loons are primitive birds dating to the time of *Tyrannosaurus rex*.

Now that through-hikers can see Katahdin, their long-sought-after destination, many are racked with anxiety. "I'm afraid of losing the simplicity and the clarity, and losing the sense of peace I've gained," said Night Sprite.

For Night Sprite, life on the trail is lived in the moment. "I don't worry about, 'Oh my God, my car payment's due; oh God, I'm late for a meeting.' I'm afraid of losing that."

She and other hikers seemed to take comfort in talking with Mailman, who through-hiked in 1994. When others learn of Mailman's experience they gather round, full of questions. Was it hard to go back to regular life afterward? Does she plan to hike the whole thing again?

She tells them it's normal to feel uneasy. "You read these books and they tell you you're probably going to be depressed, but it's so individual," she said. "It depends on the reasons you went out in the first place, and what you encountered on the hike.

"When you first get off the trail, you don't know—you feel happy, you feel sad. I've been learning in bits and pieces, and still am learn-

Easily the classiest outhouse in Maine, if not on the whole trail, is this log cabin–style outbuilding at Antlers Campsite on the shore of Lower Jo-Mary Lake in Maine. It features curtained windows, a mirror and a wash basin. Photo by John Ewing, Maine Sunday Telegram

The calm waters of Cooper Pond reflect the rolling hills along the trail in the 100-mile wilderness of Maine. Photo by John Ewing, Maine Sunday Telegram

ing a year later, the ways I benefited."

And what of the ending itself? Will reaching Katahdin be a real climax? A hiker pondered that in a register entry at the Long Pond Stream lean-to. "A dream attained is seldom as sweet as it was envisioned," mused the hiker Blind Faith.

But Kevin McDonough (King) of Glastonbury, Connecticut, had no such doubts when, from atop White Cap Mountain, 73 miles away, he got his first look at Katahdin.

"You talk about it so much, and for so long. Then you finally see it," said King. "You realize your goal is attainable. And it's kind of surreal. It's like walking in a dreamworld."

KATAHDIN, MAINE

After a final uphill push over granite boulders and pointy rock shards, Andrew Knutsen (Ack Squared) glimpsed the summit of the mighty mountain toward which he had been struggling since spring. What he saw startled him.

There must have been 60 people, maybe more, milling about the barren top of Baxter

Wildlife of the North

Much wildlife of the northern Appalachians — black bears, white-tailed deer, foxes, skunks and raccoons, for example — also is present along the Appalachian Trail as far south as Georgia. A few species, however, make their home only in the north. And though they survive by being generally elusive, an alert hiker might smell, hear or even meet them on the trail.

Maine moose

Largest member of deer family. Usually lives alone, not in herds. Poor eyesight. Keen sense of smell. Excellent hearing. In fall, feeds in ponds, bogs and lakes. Swims well, and can run up to 35 mph. Males in autumn weigh 1,000 pounds or more and become aggressive, engaging in antler-to-antler combat as they search for mates. Both bulls and cows make calling sounds in the mating season.

FIELD NOTES

Give a bull moose in rut plenty of "personal space," especially when it flattens its ears, flares its mane or holds its head high or low — all warning signs of a charge.

Fisher

About 40 inches long. Lives alone. Male associates with female only in summer during mating. Mainly a nighttime hunter, it feeds on squirrels, mice, raccoons, rabbits and some vegetation.

Spruce grouse

Thirteen to 16 inches, head to tail. Can vary in color from gray-brown to reddish brown. Lives in large tracts of conifers. Survives winter on austere diet of conifer needles.

FIELD NOTES

Its trusting behavior has earned the spruce grouse the nickname "fool's hen." Humans may get within a few feet before the bird flushes to a tree and perches.

Rock vole

About 7 inches long. Lives in small colonies in rocky places. Communicates in high-pitched sounds beyond human hearing range (also inaudible to predatory owls). Eats grass, roots, bark and seeds.

FIELD NOTES

Its haunting laughs and yodels are often compared to insane laughter.

Common loon

About 30 inches long. Prefers large lakes. Can swim long distances underwater, feeding on fish, now and again poking its bill above surface for air. Migrates to Atlantic coast east and south when ice starts to form on northern lakes.

PETE KOLSTI / Maine Sunday Telegram

Peak. "I thought there was a convention going on," said Knutsen.

It was October 1. Katahdin, Maine's tallest and most imposing mountain, wore a skirt of autumn foliage and was welcoming under a brilliant sun. No wonder everyone was out: day hikers, weekenders and, of course, through-hikers.

Amid the ruckus, Knutsen looked quietly southward at the golden landscape—at the glistening ponds and lakes and wispy clouds, at the steam rising from a paper mill's stack 20 miles away in Millinocket, the nearest town. Somehow the view helped to mute the noise.

Knutsen's mind was brimming, though not with rational thoughts. "It's more emotions—happiness and sadness," said the 40-year-old hiker, who left a job working with computers in Washington, D.C., to walk the trail.

The brawny mass that Indians called Kette-Adene, or "greatest mountain," is where the Appalachian Trail ends. It is a fitting conclusion to a rugged adventure.

Katahdin often hides its head in clouds. It was that way when Henry David Thoreau, the naturalist and writer, climbed the mountain 149 years ago. In fact, the mist prevented him from reaching the summit, which he

Framed by fall colors, a mountain looms over Pollywog Stream in the 100-mile wilderness. Photo by John Ewing, Maine Sunday Telegram

Enjoying the warmth of a campfire after a day's hike is one of the pleasures of the trail. Hiker Joyce Mailman shares a story with her fellow hikers at Potaywadjo Spring lean-to in Maine's 100-mile wilderness. Photo by John Ewing, Maine Sunday Telegram

described as "a dark isthmus...connecting the heavens with the earth."

The mountain is a stunning sight for through-hikers, a sweet payoff for the blisters and aches endured by many to get here. "Every time I see it, I feel like crying," said Henry Tanner (Screaming Coyote), a 22-year-old through-hiker from Raleigh, North Carolina.

His mother, Sally Tanner, did cry when she saw it from a car headed for a rendezvous with her son in Baxter State Park, home of Katahdin. "We came off the interstate and it just flew up," said Sally Tanner, whom hikers dubbed Mama Coyote. "I just burst into tears."

The mountain would make her want to cry for a different reason before the trip was over, but at the moment, Tanner's tears were the proud kind. Not only had her son just walked more than 2,100 hard miles, he had done so with a body that wasn't fully cooperative.

In March 1994, Henry Tanner was wrestling playfully with his college roommate when he twisted his neck. The injury created a blood clot that caused a stroke. Tanner's left side was paralyzed; one doctor said the young man might not walk again. He proved that doctor wrong by walking the Appalachian Trail.

There was already a crowd at the summit of Katahdin when Screaming Coyote took his final steps on that journey. He was easy to spot

Through-hikers pause at a scenic outlook atop Nesuntabunt Mountain for a look at the cloud-covered Katahdin, across Nahmakanta Lake. Photo by John Ewing, Maine Sunday Telegram

Predawn light reflects Katahdin in the calm waters of Daicey Pond in Maine's Baxter State Park. Photo by John Ewing, Maine Sunday Telegram

in his yellow windbreaker, his hair an unruly golden mane. His knee and a hand were a little bloody from falling on the rough pink-and-gray granite. He limped slightly. In short, he looked like most other worn-out hikers.

The crowd went silent, then someone started clapping. The applause rose to a standing ovation and coyote howls when he reached the last trail sign marking the summit.

"Wow," Screaming Coyote said, looking around self-consciously at all the wet eyes watching him. Then he caught the view beyond, and forgot about himself. "It sure is pretty up here," he said.

The private moment passed, and Screaming Coyote accepted hugs from the throng. He wished aloud that his parents would arrive; the jumble of boulders below, requiring a hand-over-hand climb, had slowed their progress. Later, the equally rough descent would threaten their safety, as we learned that evening.

After the last light had faded, at Katahdin Stream campground at the mountain's base, several through-hikers told us that Screaming Coyote's parents were still on the trail, with no flashlights or food. Screaming Coyote had come down ahead of them. He paced the parking lot in agitation.

Henry Tanner (Screaming Coyote) approaches the end of the trail atop Katahdin. Photo by John Ewing, Maine Sunday Telegram

A few hikers quickly volunteered to look for the Tanners. The search party found the couple less than two miles up the trail, in black woods. They were not hurt, just exhausted, dehydrated and hungry.

"I'd gotten up the mountain—I thought surely I'd be able to get down!" Mama Coyote said later in embarrassed relief. "That sun went down, and I just panicked."

The Tanners were not the first to be caught unprepared on Katahdin. "It happens several times a week," said Irwin Caverly, Jr., Baxter State Park's director. He said such mini-rescues are necessary for everything from sprained ankles to fatigue to heat exhaustion to people just underestimating how long it takes to hike the mountain. Sometimes mountain visits end fatally. On Labor Day weekend 1995, a 30-year-old rock climber from Massachusetts fell to his death, becoming the 18th fatality on the mountain since 1963.

Through-hikers find the challenge of Katahdin a fitting climax to their long journey. Jason Fried (Jake), a 24-year-old from Waynesburg, Pennsylvania, had joked with other hikers that the end would be not a mountain but a parking lot. "Asphalt," he said, "with your family waiting for you."

But they found that Katahdin is no myth. "This is a great place to end a trail," Fried said thankfully. "It's big. It's a fitting end."

For some, the end of the trail isn't an ending at all but a fresh beginning. In a notebook at a hikers' shelter 30 miles from the summit, a through-hiker called Houndog left this entry: "The Appalachian Trail opened my eyes to a world I never knew existed. In a way, this is not the end, but really the beginning. I hope one day to return to the Appalachian Trail and be able to feel the presence of all those I hiked with in spirit. So long."

RIGHT: *A joyful Screaming Coyote completes the trail.* Photo by John Ewing, Maine Sunday Telegram

BELOW: *Lloyd Ferriss and Joyce Mailman descend Katahdin's Knife Edge after completing their climb via the trail.* Photo by John Ewing, Maine Sunday Telegram

By Scott Huler

I obsessively watched the weather channel for nearly half an hour before the thought crossed my mind: Who cares?

It didn't make a difference whether it was going to pour all week. If it was going to be chilly, I didn't need to carry those gloves one more week before shipping them home. I live in a house now, with a closet filled with clothes and a supermarket full of food a mile away. The weather didn't make a difference. I was crushed. I felt disconnected from my surroundings, disoriented to the point of dysfunction.

I was off the trail.

People who have through-hiked the Appalachian Trail talk about the difficult adjustment when they return to what they often call "the other real life," and now I can understand why. I was on the trail only seven weeks, but the return to civilization has me stunned and hesitant, blinking as though I've just awakened.

Of course I miss the friends I made on the trail. Like summer campers, through-hikers form a tight community. We have shared something special and intense; we have formed a brotherhood, and I miss them. Less seriously, I am working hard to remember that body function noises are not as acceptable off the trail as they are out in the woods.

But what I notice most are the details. For one thing, it is so noisy here. Sitting quietly in my back yard late in the day I hear traffic, lawn mowers, radios from nearby houses and passing cars. And this is not even a particularly noisy place—this is Raleigh, where if you hear a siren it probably means that somebody put out the recycling on the wrong day and the neighbors called 911.

I miss the silence of late afternoon on the trail, when the only sound was the dripping of rain from the trees, the burbling of a brook or the laughter of a few companions.

I miss the peace of the mornings, when I

could drink coffee and stare in a way that seemed perfectly appropriate to my solitary surroundings.

I miss the connection with my environment. For seven weeks I was an intimate with the sun. I saw it rise and set every single day. I set up my tent instinctively, orienting the door toward the east for the morning sun without a conscious thought. I was out in the woods all day, yet I just knew where the sun was. Now, though I know the sun comes in my bedroom window in the morning, once I step outside the house I need a compass to find east. In my yard, it simply doesn't matter.

Most of all, though, I miss the rhythms of a day spent only walking. On the trail, walking was nothing more than a fact of life. When it was done, sleeping was peaceful and easy. I faced no choices. When following the white blazes is all you do every day, a certain peace will find you. It has to.

I now face a life that is, like everyone's, filled with trail intersections, with unmarked spots leading I don't know where, and with the awful uncertainty that accompanies a world where choice is infinite. And with all the beauty that infinite choice offers, I miss— more than I could have imagined—a world where my only choices involved where to stop for the night and which flavor of Lipton dinner to eat at each meal.

If you picture me standing, a little sadly, on a wooded hilltop where dozens of trails wander in every direction, with several maps, each of which gives me inconsistent and incomplete information about only some of the trails, you won't be far off.

But even in that I find comfort. Art, literature and song are filled with the metaphor of the journey, of the quest. I've had a little quest now, and when I came off the trail I thought that my first job would be to find a new metaphor to live by.

But as I conceive of my life now I find that the metaphor hasn't changed: Like everyone, I'm still on a quest. I'm just on the next one, and my decisions now involve which way to go. If I've learned anything from the trail it's that if you trust the universe it will find a way to guide you. I may be separated from trail magic, but I can commit myself to being open to whatever magic the universe wishes to send my way. If I have courage maybe I can even count on it.

So I address my life, I consider my metaphors, and I begin—by doing the same thing I did on the trail.

I put one foot in front of the other. And I walk.

FOR MORE INFORMATION ABOUT THE APPALACHIAN TRAIL
▲

The Appalachian Trail Conference
P.O. Box 807
Harpers Ferry, WV 25425
(304) 535–6331

ATC REGIONAL OFFICES
▲

Georgia, North Carolina and Tennessee
Morgan Sommerville
c/o U.S. Forest Service
P.O. Box 2750
Asheville, NC 28802
(704) 254–3708

Central and Southwestern Virginia
Mike Dawson
P.O. Box 10
Newport, VA 24128
(703) 544–7388

Mid-Atlantic (Shenandoah Park, VA
to Connecticut)
Karen Lutz
P.O. Box 381
Boiling Springs, PA 17007
(717) 258–5771

New England
Kevin Peterson
P.O. Box 312
Lyme, NH 03768
(603) 795–4935

RECOMMENDED READING
▲

Beeson, D.R. *In the Spirit of Adventure.*
Seymour, Tennessee: Panther Press, 1994.

Bruce, Dan. *The Thru-Hiker's Handbook.* Hot
Springs, North Carolina: The Center for
Appalachian Trail Studies, 1995.

Chase, Jim. *Backpacker Magazine's Guide to the
Appalachian Trail.* Harrisburg, Pennsylvania:
Stackpole Books, 1989.

Fisher, Ronald M. *Mountain Adventure: Explor-
ing the Appalachian Trail.* Washington, D.C.:
National Geographic Society, 1988.

Hemphill, Paul. *Me and the Boy.* New York:
Macmillan Publishing Company, 1986.

Houk, Rose. *Great Smoky Mountains National
Park: A Natural History Guide.* Boston:
Houghton Mifflin, 1993.

Logue, Frank and Victoria. *The Appalachian
Trail Backpacker.* Birmingham, Alabama:
Menasha Ridge Press, 1990.

——. *The Best of the Appalachian Trail: Day
Hikes.* Birmingham, Alabama: Menasha Ridge
Press, 1989.

——. *The Best of the Appalachian Trail:
Overnight Hikes.* Birmingham, Alabama:
Menasha Ridge Press, 1994.

MacKaye, Benton. *The New Exploration: A
Philosophy of Regional Planning.* Urbana-
Champaign, Illinois: University of Illinois Press,
1990.

Muench, David. *Uncommon Places: A Celebration
of Appalachian Trail Country.* Harpers Ferry, West
Virginia: Appalachian Trail Conference, 1991.

Ross, Cindy. *A Woman's Journey.* Harpers Ferry,
West Virginia: Appalachian Trail Conference,
1990.

Shaffer, Earl. *Walking With Spring: The First
Through-Hike of the Appalachian Trail.*
Harpers Ferry, West Virginia: Appalachian Trail
Conference, 1983.

Weidensaul, Scott. *Mountains of the Heart: A
Natural History of the Appalachians.* Golden,
Colorado: Fulcrum Publishing, 1994.

ON THE INTERNET
▲

Appalachian Trail home page
http://www.fred.net/kathy/at.html

An Appalachian Adventure
http://www.nando.net/AT/ATmain.html

Georgia Appalachian Trail Club
http://www.mindspring.com/~jvkovar/gatc/gatc.h
tml

Potomac Appalachian Trail Club
http://io.datasys.swri.edu/PATC/patc.html

Appalachian Trail in Connecticut
http://cusp.cs.yale.edu/HTML/ATCT/ATCTLINK/

Appalachian Mountain Club
http://www.lehigh.edu/ludas/public/www-data/
amc.html

Piedmont Appalachian Trail Hikers
http://www.ansouth.net/~dchildre/path.htm